GUDERIAN

MILITARY PROFILES

SERIES EDITOR
Dennis E. Showalter, Ph.D.
Colorado College

*Instructive summaries for general and expert
readers alike, volumes in the Military Profiles
series are essential treatments of significant and
popular military figures drawn from world history,
ancient times through the present.*

GUDERIAN

Panzer Pioneer or Myth Maker?

Russell A. Hart

Potomac Books, Inc.
Washington, D.C.

Library of Congress Cataloging-in-Publication Data
Hart, Russell A.
   Guderian : Panzer pioneer or myth maker? / Russell A. Hart.—1st ed.
      p. cm.—(Military profiles)
   Includes bibliographical references and index.
   ISBN 1-57488-809-9 (alk. paper)—ISBN 1-57488-810-2 (pbk. : alk. paper)
   1. Guderian, Heinz, 1888–1954. 2. Generals—Germany—Biography. 3. Germany. Heer—Biography. 4. Germany. Heer—Armored troops—History. 5. World War, 1939–1945—Tank warfare. I. Title. II. Series.

U55.G8H28 2006
358'.18092—dc22
[B]

                                        2005055226

ISBN-10 1-57488-809-9 HC
ISBN-13 978-1-57488-809-6 HC
ISBN-10 1-57488-810-2 PB
ISBN-13 978-1-57488-810-2 PB

Potomac Books, Inc.
22841 Quicksilver Drive
Dulles, Virginia 20166

First Edition

10 9 8 7 6 5 4 3 2 1

Contents

Maps

Preface

I have incurred many debts of gratitude during completion of this biography of Heinz Guderian. I would like to thank Alex Lassner for sharing his research on the military aspects of the German annexation of Austria in 1938. I would also like to thank Geoff Megargee, Jörg Muth, Gerhard Weinberg, Dennis Showalter, and Wick Murray for their insights into Guderian's personality, relationships, and career. I must also acknowledge the assistance and advice of Mark Reardon, which has been indispensable. Thanks also go to Jim Gates, Michael Pavkovic', Jim McNaughton, Dan Mortensen, Rob Rush, Tom Hughes, and David Zabecki for advice, friendship, and encouragement. As ever I am indebted to my brother, Stephen Hart, and especially my wife, Allison Gough, for their valuable input and support. At Potomac Books, Inc., I would like to thank Paul Merzlak, Rick Russell, and Laura Hymes for their confidence, guidance, and camaraderie, without which this project would never have reached fruition. I would also like to thank Donald Frazier for his valuable work on the maps. Special *mahalo* goes to my program director at Hawai'i Pacific University, Michael Pavelec, and to the generous support of several HPU Trustees Scholarly Endeavors Program grants, without which this project could never have been completed. At HPU, I would also like to thank Ralph Kam and Stefanie Sasaki for their assistance. Any errors of fact that remain are my responsibility alone.

Chronology

1888	Born in Kulm, West Prussia to Prussian officer Friedrich Guderian and his wife Clara Kirchhoff.
1907	Enters the Imperial German Army after attending cadet schools in Karlsruhe and Berlin.
1908	Commissioned as a second lieutenant in the 10th Light Infantry Battalion at Goslar.
1912	Communications training at Coblenz.
1913	Marries Margarete Doerne. They subsequently had two sons.
1913	Enters the *Kriegsakademie* in Berlin.
1914	Joins 5th Cavalry Division as communications officer.
1914, Aug.	Son, Heinz Günter Guderian, born.
1915	Appointed intelligence officer with Fifth Army.
1916	Becomes senior intelligence officer, Fourth Army, Flanders.
1918, Feb.	Officially inducted into the Greater German General Staff.
1918, May	Appointed Quartermaster, XXXVIII Reserve Corps.
1918, Sept.	Chief operations officer, German Military Mission attached to the Austro-Hungarian Army. Second son, Kurt Guderian, born.
1919	Assigned to Central (later Northern) Command, Frontier Guard Service East.

1919, June	Appointed Second Staff Officer, Iron Division.
1920	Transferred from General Staff, appointed captain, and given a company command in the 10th Light Infantry Battalion of the Provisional *Reichswehr*.
1922	Transferred to the Inspectorate of Transport Troops and assigned as the chief staff officer of the 7th Bavarian Motor Transport Battalion in Munich.
1922	First articles on armor published.
1924	Appointed Instructor, 2d Infantry Division at Stettin.
1927, Jan.	Promoted to major.
1927, Oct.	Posted to Transport Section of the Operations Department of the Truppenamt.
1928	Founds Tactical Instruction Department, Transport Section, Operations Department.
1930	Commander, 3d Motor Transport Battalion.
1931	Appointed Chief of Staff of the Inspectorate of Transportation Troops.
1933	Attends first Nazi Party meetings and rallies.
1934	Appointed Chief of Staff to the Commander of the Motor Combat Troops.
1934	Promoted to colonel.
1935, Oct.	Appointed commander of the 2d Panzer Division.
1936	Promoted to major general.
1937	Publishes *Achtung! Panzer!*
1938, Mar.	Guderian's 2d Panzer Division participated in the anschluss of Austria.
1938	Promoted to lieutenant general and given command of XVI Corps.
1938, Oct.	Participated in the occupation of the Sudetenland.
1938, Nov.	Promoted to General of Armored Troops and appointed Chief of Mobile Troops.

1939, Sept.	Leads XIX Motorized Corps in conquest of Poland.
1940	Participates in planning for invasion of the West.
1940, May	19th Motorized Corps successfully penetrates the Ardennes and advances to the Channel coast near Amiens, isolating the British Expeditionary Force.
1940, June	19th Motorized Corps participates in German offensive across the Somme. Advances to the Swiss border, encircling and eliminating the French Army group defending the Maginot Line.
1940, July	Promoted to colonel-general.
1941, June	2d Panzer Group spearheads the advance of Army Group Center.
1941, July	Receives Oak Leaves to the Knight's Cross.
1941, Aug.	Completes the encirclement of Kiev.
1941, Oct.	2d Panzer Army advances via Bryansk toward Moscow.
1941, Dec.	Advance is halted at the gates of Moscow. Soviet winter counteroffensive forces 2d Panzer Army to retreat.
1941, Dec.	Relieved of command for repeated disobedience of orders and assigned to the officer reserve at Zossen.
1942	Convalesces and spends his time hunting for an estate to acquire.
1942, Oct.	Acquired rural estate at Gut Diepenhof in the Wartheland using bribes received from Hitler. Resumes traditional activities of the Junker elite.
1943	Appointed Inspector General of Armored Troops.
1944, June	Recommends that von Stauffenberg (the dynamo behind the anti-Hitler conspiracy) be appointed to Hitler's headquarters.
1944, 20 July	Disappears hunting on his rural estate on the same afternoon that von Stauffenberg's assassination attempt on Hitler's life fails.

1944, 21 July	Appointed acting Chief of the General Staff by Hitler.
1944, Aug.	Pushes for Nazification of the army and joins a special honor court of the army that dishonorably discharged assassination conspirators from the military, paving the way for their torture and execution by the Gestapo.
1945, Feb.	Orchestrates spoiling attack at Arnswalde that delays final Soviet drive on Berlin.
1945, Mar.	Sent on six weeks medical leave by Hitler.
1945, May	After receiving double his normal monthly bribe, returns to his position as Inspector General of Armored Troops one week before the war ends.
1945, May	Becomes a U.S. prisoner of war.
1948	Released from imprisonment.
1951	Publishes autobiography, *Memories of a Soldier*.
1952	Autobiography published in English as *Panzer Leader*. It became one of the most widely read English-language memoirs of the Second World War.
1954	Dies.

GUDERIAN

Introduction

HEINZ GUDERIAN has been lionized by many as the legendary father of the German armored force and brilliant practitioner of *Blitzkrieg* maneuver warfare. Guderian created this legend with his own highly influential, yet self-serving and distorted memoir, which remains one of the most widely read accounts of the Second World War.[1] Unfortunately, too many of Guderian's biographers have accepted Guderian's view of his accomplishments without sufficient critical scrutiny.[2] The result has been an undeserved hagiography of Guderian. While undoubtedly a great military figure, Guderian was a man of appreciable ego and ambition—a volatile, impetuous, and difficult personality determined to achieve his vision of a war-winning armored force, irrespective of the consequences. He proved naive enough to fall under the sway of Hitler and National Socialism, yet arrogant enough to believe, late in the war, that he could save Germany from inevitable defeat despite Hitler. In spite of his later disapproval of Hitler, he proved unwilling either to participate in attempts to remove him or to denounce as traitors the conspirators that did. In the end, he proved to be a man prepared to distort the truth in order to establish his place in history. In doing so, he denigrated the myriad important contributions of other

Germans as he took personal credit for what were, in reality, collective accomplishments. He succeeded in creating a legend that has endured long after his death. This brief biography begins to put the record straight by endeavoring to place Guderian's career and accomplishments into sharper and more accurate relief. It seeks the real Heinz Guderian, not the man of legend.

1

Guderian's Youth and Early Military Career, 1888–1914

H EINZ GUDERIAN was born on 17 June 1888 in Kulm, West Prussia, to Friedrich and Clara Guderian, middle-class Prussians. His father and grandfathers were Prussian officers, and growing up in a military family profoundly shaped Guderian's character. He spent much of his childhood in garrison towns and as an adolescent naturally aspired to follow in the footsteps of his forebears. Consequently, in 1903 Guderian left home to board at military cadet schools first in Baden and then in Berlin. In these institutions, Guderian was infused with the Prussian military tradition and its demands for flexibility, ingenuity, and individual initiative. He proved himself to be a quick study and consistently performed in the top of his classes. By the time he had reached his late teens at the Military Academy in Metz in 1907, Guderian had already begun to exhibit the vigor, independence, and ambition that dominated his adult life.[1] At the academy he demonstrated great determination, optimism, and industry, traits that would dominate his future military career. Yet, he also exhibited stubborn independence: he fared poorly in his final exam because he rejected the prescribed solution he had been taught and instead presented an original tactical response that failed to impress the examiners.[2] It was this obstinate and often arrogant independence that defined Guderian's persona and helped establish him as a significant historical figure.

In February 1907 Guderian became an officer candidate in the 10th Hanoverian Light Infantry Battalion, commanded by his father. Successfully completing his probation, Guderian became a second lieutenant in January 1908. He enjoyed the traditional elite activities that officers enjoyed—hunting, shooting, riding, theater, and dances—activities that accorded with Guderian's sense of his family's privileged past.

As an officer candidate, Guderian began to exhibit a critical character: he often complained about the German military system and what he perceived as its weaknesses. This critical eye reflected a healthy skepticism, though at heart Guderian was an inveterate optimist. Possessing a sharp intellect, Guderian immersed himself in the study of military history and possessed an outstanding memory that often proved to be an asset in his career. Always, his father remained his role model—a classic exemplar of the loyal, obedient, dedicated, professional Prussian military officer. Guderian proved mature beyond his age and was so focused on his studies and professional development that he remained aloof and developed few close friends—traits that likewise characterized his life. He did develop a good friendship with another young officer aspirant, Bodewin Keitel, and the Keitel family subsequently played a special role in Guderian's future personal and professional life.

As an officer cadet Guderian also first displayed the aversion to senior authority figures that would haunt his military career. His ego also clearly developed; he came to see himself as more dedicated than his fellow officer aspirants and expressed criticism of what he saw as their lack of professionalism. While he was undoubtedly among the best of his peers, his self-image reflected ego tinged with arrogance. That egoism was revealed when Guderian, convinced that he was surrounded by mediocrity, demanded a transfer to the elite of the Imperial German officer corps—the General Staff. Thus even at the beginning of his military career, Guderian's quest for excellence and his ambition and egotism had already emerged. He would carry these traits with him throughout his life.

In 1909 Guderian fell in love with Margarete "Gretel" Doerne. But opposition to their relationship from Gretel's father (who thought them too young) provided the impetus for Guderian to seek escape from the claustrophobic confines of Goslar, where he was now stationed. Courses were available for training on machine guns or in signals. Guderian favored the former, but his father saw potential in the new wireless radios that had recently been introduced and counseled his son to take the communications course. It was a prescient decision that would have profound consequences for Guderian's military career. On 1 October 1912 Guderian joined the Radio Company of the 3d Telegraph Battalion at Coblenz. Here he also took preparatory classes for the Imperial War Academy. Applying himself with his usual impressive diligence, he quickly qualified as a French interpreter and he became virtually fluent in English. He passed the War Academy entrance exams on the first try and became the youngest, at twenty-five, of 168 officers selected to attend a three-year War Academy staff course in Berlin. On 5 October 1913, Guderian entered the prestigious *Kriegsakademie* in Berlin. His obvious intellect, diligence, and aptitude quickly led his fellow academy students to dub him "*Schnelle Heinz*" (Quick Henry).[3]

These career accomplishments meanwhile offset the objections of Gretel's parents and on 1 October 1913, Guderian and Gretel married. At the War Academy he demonstrated an idiosyncratic blend of studied thought, boundless energy, and alarming impetuosity that subsequently made Guderian infamous. Gretel proved a valuable counterpoint for Guderian, calming him and prodding him on to a more conventional path. Gretel clearly saw her husband as a great man and dedicated herself to helping Guderian realize his full potential.[4]

Guderian's chief instructor was Colonel Graf Rüdiger von der Goltz, an energetic and charismatic senior officer who soon had Guderian spellbound. (Their paths would intersect again later, at a decisive moment when Guderian stood at a crossroads in his career at the end of the Great War.) Guderian initially studied military history and tactics before moving on to acquire knowledge of the various combat arms. Thus as war clouds gathered during the summer of 1914, Guderian joined a field artillery unit. The declaration of German war mobilization on 1 August, however, terminated his studies, and Guderian assumed command of the 3d Heavy Wireless Station, 5th Cavalry Division attached to the I Cavalry Corps, Second Army.

The fundamental qualities that Guderian demonstrated throughout his life were thus forged in his youth and early military career. Guderian was an inveterate optimist, yet subject to sudden and wild mood swings; bad news could throw him into despondency. His intellect, acute powers of observation, and outspoken critical nature were equally evident. His first major operational field maneuvers with a wireless detachment during the spring of 1914 led him to write a scathing critique of what he perceived as the misuse of the communications equipment and personnel. Wireless communication remained in its infancy and many practicalities of its proper employment had yet to be fully ironed out. Low down on the procurement ladder and with few strong advocates for the technology he specialized in, Guderian chafed at the institutional and political obstacles that prevented this arm of service from realizing its potential. It certainly would not be the last time that Guderian would chafe at institutional barriers as the rivalries of the European great powers threw the world into the catastrophe that was the Great War.[5]

2

Guderian and the Great War, 1914–1918

G UDERIAN'S EXPERIENCES during the Great War were central to his future military career and his subsequent advocacy of armored forces and mechanization. In serving as a staff officer, Guderian largely avoided the slaughter in the trenches on the Western Front. This allowed him to develop a detached view of the course of operations and to analyze and to understand the character of the Great War and hence the reasons for German defeat. He used this opportunity to contemplate potential means of preventing a future recurrence of static warfare, believing as he did that future conflict was inevitable.[1]

Guderian's wireless detachment supported a cavalry division that sought to breach the Marne River at the forefront of the German Schlieffen Plan offensive that sought to outflank Paris quickly and knock France out of the Great War. Guderian's unit quickly advanced through the Ardennes—a place he would return to some twenty-six years later in 1940. The relative ease with which the Germans supplied their advance to the Meuse through difficult terrain left a lasting impression on Guderian and later gave him confidence that this accomplishment could be repeated. Yet, the relentless pace of operations soon began to take its toll on his small wireless detachment.

Guderian quickly developed his own command style, which endured throughout his career: he led from the front and thus repeatedly came close to combat during those early days of mobile warfare. However, tenacious Anglo-French resistance and the inevitable friction of war soon wrecked the German timetable as the German advance faltered during the Battle for the Marne. The exposed German cavalry spearheads now found themselves threatened with annihilation and were forced to retire. During this retreat Guderian's signals unit got caught up in frontline fighting near Chéry and Guderian was almost captured.[2] It would not be the last time that recklessness would almost derail his military career.

It was during these taxing times that Guderian began to criticize harshly his divisional commander while lavishly praising his junior officers. This tendency to hold his superiors to the most exacting (and sometimes impossible) standards while exhibiting beneficent paternalism toward his subordinates would characterize Guderian's command relationships throughout his military career.[3]

In September 1914 Guderian transferred to the Fourth Army on the Flanders front and took command of the 14th Wireless Section. Once again he witnessed the stumbling halt of the German war machine and the emergence of trench warfare. A progressive reformer, Guderian eagerly embraced the operational debut of the airplane and perceived its potential for intelligence gathering and facilitating communications. He was thus one of a only a handful of army officers who flew during 1914 in an effort both to appreciate the military utility of aircraft and to obtain a better understanding of the course of operations. It was on the Ypres front, on 22 April 1915, that Guderian witnessed the premature German deployment of mustard gas.[4] The lesson he learned regarding the hasty employment of a new weapon before its full development stayed with him throughout his career.

Presently Guderian received promotion to intelligence officer— an appointment that clearly reflected his superiors' assessments of his keen intellect—and moved to the Fifth Army headquarters on the Verdun front. Here, he witnessed first-hand the appalling consequences of the German effort to shatter the French military in the brutal *materialschlacht* (battle of attrition) that was the 1916 Battle for Verdun. In this attritional struggle the forces of both sides eschewed any pretense at mobility. Guderian helped write operational analyses of the offensive's failure, and the conclusions he drew—that artillery firepower could not neutralize an entrenched enemy and that only maneuver could offer a less costly means of victory—would profoundly shape his subsequent ideas and his career. Guderian's subsequent disdain for the artillery apparently had its roots in his perception of its failure at Verdun.[5]

In July 1916 Guderian returned to the Fourth Army in Flanders as its senior intelligence officer. He was in Flanders when the British first used tanks on the Somme on 15 September 1916. Like most German army officers of the time, Guderian showed little interest in what was just one of many new weapons and tactical adaptations constantly introduced by both sides in an attempt to break the impasse of trench warfare.[6]

Forced on the defensive, Germany developed sophisticated and elaborate defenses in depth on the Western Front, adopting the doctrine of "delaying defense," an economical measure in attritional warfare.[7] Guderian would later vehemently denounce this defensive doctrine, only to find himself practicing it during his most trying times as a field commander, in the depths of Russia in December 1941.[8] The savage casualty rate on the Western Front, particularly among officers, opened avenues for promotion that would have been impossible for Guderian in peacetime. Moreover, as a staff intelligence officer, Guderian faced a substantially lower risk of being killed or maimed than frontline combat officers. The urgent demand for new staff officers saw individuals such as Guderian whose staff training had been interrupted by the outbreak of war being dispatched to new "crash" wartime General Staff courses and a simultaneous series of attachments to various combat commands and branches of service to broaden their expertise.

Guderian was serving on the Aisne in April 1917 when the French first abortively used tanks, and once again this event failed to elicit any more interest from Guderian than the previous British employment. Operational necessities, however, prevented Guderian from returning to his prewar staff training until January 1918, when he finally attended a General Staff officers training course at Sedan. On

28 February 1918 Guderian became a full-fledged officer of the elite Greater German General Staff. As ever, he reviewed his staff training with a critical eye: at a later date he would shrewdly assess it as "too narrow."[9] Indeed, it lacked a technical focus and failed to examine sufficiently the impact of technology on the modern battlefield.[10]

On 20 November 1917, massed Allied employment of tanks led to an operational breakthrough on the main German Hindenburg Line at Cambrai in a single morning. This event augured the future strategic potential of armor on the modern battlefield. Again, nothing suggests that Guderian took more than a passing interest in these momentous battlefield developments. He was preoccupied with other developments. For the German army had been developing its own solution to the intractability of trench warfare in the form of storm troop tactics.[11] Evolved out of traditional German military tenets of offense and maneuver and buttressed by experience on the Eastern Front, where mobile operations had often persisted, the Germans began using these new techniques in the west on 21 March 1918, during the "Peace Offensives"—all out storm troop attacks intended to crush the Anglo-French armies before the American Expeditionary Force could arrive in strength to turn the tide of the war on the Western Front. These attacks rapidly recouped all previously lost territory.[12] Storm troop tactics relied heavily on decentralized local command and initiative and thus demanded superior communications. These developments rejuvenated the signals corps, bringing a substantial injection of new resources as well as new procedures to ensure effective command communications.

Guderian was only peripherally involved in these developments. Nevertheless, in assisting the preparations for these offensives, Guderian studied storm troop tactics and the resurgent efficacy of mobile operations. This training reconfirmed the main lesson he had drawn from Verdun—the necessity for a return to mobile operations. Yet, during May 1918 he became the quartermaster for the XXXVIII Reserve Corps and became suffused in the humdrum world of logistics on a quiet sector of the front. His wartime experience and ability were obviously not deemed sufficient for him to participate in the greatest German endeavor of the war. But as a corps quartermaster, Guderian did gain some very useful logistical experience, particularly

regarding the limitations that supply imposed on offensive operations. His corps did finally participate in the Peace Offensives, but
only peripherally, as it provided flank protection for a subsidiary attack across the Aisne River. This attack achieved surprise on 27 May
1918 and advanced 14 miles in a single day, the longest German
advance on the Western Front since the onset of trench warfare.[13]
Subsequently the corps participated in the Metz offensive that began
on 9 June, but this gained far less success and encountered stiff French
resistance, including France's first *en masse* employment of tanks.
With armored support the French threw back Guderian's corps and
recaptured all the lost ground. Here, for the first time, during the
summer of 1918, Guderian came to appreciate the powerful effect
that concentrated armored support could have on the modern battlefield.

As the tide turned and the Allies drove back a demoralized German army exhausted by continuous offensive action, Guderian's corps
was committed to bolstering the sagging defense during early August. But nothing—certainly not Guderian's efforts to maintain adequate supply—could arrest the dramatic decline of German offensive power and the irresistible loss of terrain. Guderian was taxed to
the limit in long days of grueling work, trying to maintain sufficient
provision for the exhausted and increasingly shaky frontline troops.
Guderian got another taste of retrograde defense as his corps fell back
during mid-August into the Siegfried Line defenses, a task completed
by mid-September 1918.[14]

At this juncture, Guderian was suddenly posted as chief operations officer to the German Military Mission attached to the Austro-
Hungarian army fighting in Italy. This important appointment
indicated that his superiors held Guderian's administrative abilities
in high regard. Yet he arrived in Italy to hear the news of the crushing Austrian defeat at Vittorio Veneto, which led Germany's ally to
seek an exit from an obviously lost war. Guderian's eternal optimism
nevertheless left him out of touch with events, as he naively believed
that the war would continue. It would not be the last time that his
optimism would blind him to the larger strategic reality. He continued to believe that only by further battlefield successes could the
Central Powers wrest acceptable peace terms from the Allies. It was

thus with dismay that on 30 October 1918, Guderian found himself the junior member of a two-person delegation dispatched to Trent to liaise with the Austrian-Italian Armistice Commission, only to find the German attendance rebuffed by the Italians. But what most preoccupied Guderian, the monarchist and nationalist, about this situation was the spread of communist sentiments among the defeated Austrian troops and the simultaneous dissolution of their discipline. The path to inglorious defeat thus proved an especially harsh one for Guderian.

From *Kaiserheer* to *Reichswehr*, 1919–1929

As UNPLEASANT as things were for Guderian in September and October 1918, he leapt from the frying pan into the fire when he left northern Italy and returned to Berlin in November; as the German military collapsed on the Western Front, revolution swept the Second Reich, the Kaiser abdicated, and a hastily constituted provisional government requested—and received—an armistice on 11 November.[1] Guderian bitterly lamented the dissolution of the empire, bemoaning the fact that Bismarck's great accomplishments now lay in ruins.[2] He was particularly appalled by the collapse of social and political order, the disintegration of military discipline, and the opprobrium that embittered civilians heaped on a defeated army. This dramatic decline in the status of the military in German society gravely offended Guderian's sense of military honor. But most significantly of all, it was the spread of Marxist socialism amid the military rank-and-file that horrified him. An elitist conservative, he remained deeply distrustful of the soldiers' and sailors' Councils that appeared that winter and feared the destabilizing chaos of coup attempts, which marked the painful transition from authoritarian empire to liberal-representative Weimar Republic. Indeed, Guderian saw communism as the archenemy of everything German. The approach of Soviet and Polish armies toward the eastern boundaries of Germany, particularly his ancestral homeland of Prussia, and the increasing support for and militancy of the socialist parties in Germany left him very fearful for the future.[3] His hatred of Bolshevism, which remained one of the constants of his life, would later help draw Guderian into a pact with Adolf Hitler and National Socialism.

Loyal to a military that was then in the process of dissolution, Captain Guderian accepted in early 1919 a new assignment, serving on the staff of the central command of the newly constituted Eastern Frontier Guard Service. This was a new government organ constituted by Field Marshal Hindenburg to control and coordinate the many disparate *Freikorps* paramilitary units then being formed by enterprising patriotic officers to defend Germany's vulnerable eastern frontiers against approaching Polish and Soviet forces.[4] The crisis that engulfed the nation in 1919 undoubtedly hardened Guderian's attitudes. A traditionalist at heart, Guderian held dear the core value of the Prussian officer corps: that of being an apolitical servant of the state. But Guderian believed that if the state itself was in disarray and degenerating into chaos, an officer must act to save the state—even from itself, if necessary. Ignoring the manifest failures of the Imperial German politico-military leadership, Guderian romanticized the "good old days" of the gifted statesman Otto von Bismarck.[5] He also began to yearn for the emergence of a talented, strong national leader—another Bismarck—who would rescue Germany from itself.

Ideologically, therefore, Guderian found a hospitable home in the *Freikorps*, which was full of nationalists, patriots, militarists, and conservatives who coalesced around the central founding principle of the Frontier Guard, fear of communism. The *Freikorps* movement had its genesis in the bloody and brutal paramilitary suppression of the Spartakist communist uprisings of early 1919.[6] Guderian felt at home with the leadership and values of the *Freikorps* and shared its constituent's dismay at the collapse of the empire, of the military, and of general order. Its members saw it as their patriotic duty to use arms—ruthlessly, if necessary—to restore order and return the military to its proper place in society and, thus, to exorcise the communist threat.

Guderian's career became inextricably intertwined with one of
the earliest and most effective of the *Freikorps* formations—the Iron
Brigade (later Division)—constituted from Eastern Front veterans
who defied the new provisional government's orders to evacuate both
conquered Russian territory and the territory of the newly reconstituted Polish nation-state. Many *Freikorps* units decided to stay and
continue to fight Germany's opponents alongside Baltic nationalists
and anti-Bolshevik Russian White Alliance forces. In March 1919
Guderian joined the Frontier Guard Service's Northern Command
where the most dedicated *Freikorps* troops gravitated with the intention of defending the ancestral lands of Prussia against the Bolshevik
advance into the Baltic States. The Iron Division was in the thick of
the fighting here under a charismatic theater commander, Major-
General Rüdiger von der Goltz, Guderian's former instructor at the
War Academy. Guderian soon found himself serving as the regular
army's official representative on the staff of the Iron Division.[7]

What remained of the *Kaiserheer* (Imperial German Army) remained deeply ambivalent about these patriotic freebooters but could
not dispense with them until a new army was constituted. The military thought it could wrest better peace terms from the victorious
Allies through feat of arms on the battlefield, so it unofficially sanctioned the *Freikorps*. However, while both the Allied powers and the
German government secretly approved of the anticommunist goals
of the *Freikorps,* they could not openly endorse and support such
military operations against the Bolsheviks. It was in this very narrow
political room for maneuver that the division and Guderian operated.

On 2 June 1919, Guderian joined the Iron Division as its second
General Staff officer. This move was intended to stiffen General Staff
control over the independently inclined von der Goltz. It was a daunting appointment for a still relatively junior officer just thirty years old.
Unfortunately, Guderian would disappoint his superiors as his anti-
communism soon overcame his orders to reassert army control over
the Iron Division. For he empathized with their defense of his Prussian
homeland against the mortal danger he perceived in communism.

The Iron Division waged a short, ruthless campaign that secured
Lithuania and pushed into Latvia, operating, albeit sporadically, with
White Russian and Baltic nationalist forces opposing the Bolsheviks.

Traditional German disdain for Slavs, however, precluded greater cooperation with these anticommunist forces. In its advance on Riga, moreover, the division committed numerous atrocities as part of its ideologically driven mission to "cleanse and clean," culminating in the so-called Rape of Riga.[8] It is inconceivable that Guderian, as a senior staff officer, could have remained ignorant of such war crimes, and his keen intellect must surely have recognized the short-sightedness of such actions. The atrocities not only alienated native Latvians and other Balts but also forced the Allies' hand against the Iron Division. It is hardly surprising, therefore, that Guderian completely ignored these ugly events in his memoirs.[9]

It was against this backdrop, on 28 June 1919, that the new Weimar government accepted the Treaty of Versailles that emasculated the German army, mandating its reduction to 100,000 ground troops by 3 March 1920. Hans von Seeckt, the new commander-in-chief designate, now tried to force von der Goltz to abandon Riga (in compliance with the peace terms) and in doing so compelled Guderian to choose between military obedience and his sense of patriotism. Not for the last time in his career, Guderian disobeyed higher authority. For Guderian—like so many other military officers—bitterly opposed the peace terms, which he saw a draconian and unfair. On 6 July, von Seeckt ordered the Iron Division to withdraw from Riga. Yet, quixotically, Guderian continued to believe that somehow the Iron Division's continuing military operations could transform the strategic picture! Here Guderian demonstrated the strategic myopia that characterized his entire military career. His words to his wife in a letter of 16 October, "show strength and never give in" (one might add "irrespective of the consequences") are an apt summary of Guderian's military career.[10]

Resigned to the fact he could not serve the government that had signed the humiliating Versailles *Diktat* (dictated peace), Guderian crept toward political revolt. Now acting operations officer (the division's first General Staff officer having already been recalled for being politically unreliable), Guderian plotted the division's "defection" to the White Russian forces then combating the Bolsheviks. Guderian's headstrong independent-mindedness led him to allow his political views to overcome his military training in this matter. With

Guderian's full approval, von der Goltz and the divisional staff defied explicit entrainment orders to return to Germany on 23 August.[11]

Guderian later claimed that "we acted for the best, for our country and our people."[12] Yet Guderian put his military career on the line—for he was an active ringleader in a military mutiny! His superiors were dismayed at his disloyalty, although many senior officers felt themselves similarly divided between loyalty to the German army and sympathy with the *Freikorps*. Consequently, he was offered a second chance, an opportunity to redeem himself. He was peremptorily recalled from the Iron Division; the Army High Command exhibited a willingness to overlook, but not forgive, his transgression.[13]

This incident demonstrated Guderian's inclination toward extremist militarist movements, his independence of thought and action, and his willingness to defy higher authority. Even when back in East Prussia at the Frontier Guard Command headquarters, Guderian continued to lobby for what was clearly a lost cause. The *Freikorps* struggle in the Baltic was doomed to failure, a conclusion any dispassionate observer could have seen. But Guderian was too blinded by ideological antipathy, patriotic passion, and simple optimism to see reality. This strategic myopia contributed to his inability to comprehend current and future political developments. These were character flaws that plagued his entire military career.

The General Staff could not forgive Guderian's disobedience, and in September 1919 he was posted to the 10th Brigade of the new provisional *Reichswehr* (as the military of the Weimar Republic had become known) in Hannover, well away from the turbulent eastern frontier. Further punishment came in January 1920 when he was transferred from the elite General Staff and consigned to a regular officer post—a company command in the 10th Light Infantry Battalion at Goslar.[14] This was, of course, his father's old battalion and the transfer was obviously no coincidence; the intent was clearly to allow Guderian to regain his footing by returning him to old, familiar surroundings, where he would fall back on the comforting daily routines of regimental soldiering.

While he was retained in the army's truncated *Reichswehr* officer corps (his strength of character alone afforded him that privilege), he was demoted from the General Staff. It is ironic, to say the least, that it was the very punishment for disobedience that set Guderian on a brand new course in his military career and lead him to far greater things. Reverting to the time-old traditions of regimental officership removed—at least temporarily—the ideological nationalism that had engulfed Guderian as all that he knew had crashed into ruins around him. His superiors accomplished their objective of "cooling and soothing" the hotheaded Guderian, yet such actions produced utterly unforeseen consequences.

The "cooling" ensured that Guderian's loyalty held firm during the March 1920 Kapp Putsch by von der Goltz and residual *Freikorps* elements. Now Guderian's loyalty to the state, for which he (like many Germans) held little affection held firm and he denounced his former colleagues who sought to overthrow the republic. This coup attempt and others, however, further reinforced his negative attitude toward the "cowardice, stupidity, and weakness of the lamentable" Weimar Republic.[15] Guderian despised Weimar for "selling out" Germany, and as a staunch monarchist, he distrusted the alien representative, democratic Republic that he and so many other Germans came to believe the victors had imposed on Germany.

Guderian meanwhile demonstrated his progressive and energetic character as a light infantry commander by whipping his company into tiptop condition. Despite his success in this and despite his protestations to the contrary in his autobiography, it is likely that he hungered to return to the General Staff.[16] In 1922 Guderian found himself transferred from the combat arms to a staff position in a support service—the Inspectorate of Transport Troops. The unit in question was the 7th Bavarian Motor Transport Battalion, one of seven such units in the *Reichswehr* that provided transport services in their respective military districts.

Guderian was likely transferred for two reasons. First, the transfer would be further punishment for his earlier disobedience. Guderian suspected that this was the real motive behind the transfer. Like most Prussian officers, Guderian held the combat arms in high regard and the support echelons in disdain. That Guderian perceived this appointment as a demotion is clear in the fact that he failed to take up the new post at the designated time. He would claim in his memoirs that there had been a "communications mix-up" and that he had never received the order. While plausible, this version of events is almost certainly disingenuous. What is known is that Guderian was dismayed, not overjoyed, at the prospect of serving in a transport battalion and vocally conveyed his dissatisfaction to anyone who would listen. The appointment was unsuitable for an officer of Guderian's ambition: it put him in a backwater from which he feared he could never escape. Thus the greatest irony of Guderian's military career was that it was this unwanted appointment that opened up new vistas for him.

In fact, Guderian could not be cajoled into accepting the appointment until he had received reassurances, blandishments, and vague promises that he would be employed directly under the Inspector of Transport Troops after gaining some practical expertise in transport operations at the motor battalion. The *Truppenamt* (troops office) stroked Guderian's ego in a letter of 16 January 1922, calling the appointment a "special recognition."[17] The insincerity of this solicitation is suggested by the letter's emphasis that this appointment required an officer of particular tact and understanding—hardly traits that Guderian had exhibited so far in his military career. One therefore cannot escape the conclusion that the appointment was indeed intended as another cooling off appointment; after all, Germany remained wracked with political turmoil and it is likely that the *Truppenamt* was aware of the personal contacts Guderian had continued to maintain within the *Freikorps* movement.[18]

The second likely reason for the appointment was the technical experience Guderian had gained serving as a staff signals officer during the Great War. Guderian was among a select group of officers that had staff, communications, and technical training. If he was to be punished by demotion to a service branch, it might as well be in a post in which his training, skills, and experience could best be put to use—the transport corps was the ideal solution.

That Guderian interpreted his transfer as a humiliating demotion is evident in his serious contemplation of resigning from the military. But his sense of duty and the need to support his family ultimately made him accept, and so he went off to Munich. Yet he was delighted to find in his new battalion commander, Major Oswald

Lutz, a kindred spirit.[19] An officer of keen intellect and a progressive reformer like Guderian, Lutz also was similarly ambitious. But he was a smoother and shrewder operator than the more temperamental Guderian. They would soon forge an excellent partnership and cordial friendship.

Yet Guderian would receive a shock after completing his familiarization training with the motor transport battalion and reporting to the personal staff of General Tschischwitz's Transport Troop Command for service. Although the *Truppenamt* had led him to believe he would be organizing motorized troops, he discovered that it was his previous logistical skills that the Transport Troop Command looked on as most valuable. Thus he was put to work on supply tasks, to his great dismay and indignation. While an able administrator, the ambitious Guderian had no desire to devote his abilities to logistical work. The prospect so appalled him that he took the unusual step of formally appealing the assignment. That his appeal was rejected demonstrates how the promises that had induced him to take the appointment were nothing more than blandishments. Undaunted by this setback, the intractable Guderian next filed for a return to the 10th Light Infantry Battalion. The request was rebuffed, this time with a reprimand, and Guderian was ordered in no uncertain terms to get on with the task to which he had been assigned.

It is ironic that Guderian desperately sought to extricate himself from the one appointment that, more than any other, would lay the foundation for his subsequent military greatness. Rebuffed and reprimanded, his ego deflated, Guderian finally settled down to motor transport logistics, an experience that certainly increased his understanding of the technical limitations of contemporary automobiles. No one—Guderian least of all—could have foreseen the profound consequences of posting a young German captain to an obscure motor transport unit in 1922. Throwing himself into the task with his tireless energy, Guderian rapidly mastered the intricacies of transport logistics. In his spare time he immersed himself in studying transportation, motorization, and mechanization. Most important, he kept clear of politics during 1923, a turbulent year that saw coup, counter-coup, and the French occupation of the Ruhr.

In his memoir Guderian writes that it was while he was serving on the staff of the Motor Transport Troop command, specifically in his study of the movement of motorized units in mobile operations, that his attention was first drawn to tanks. Because the German army had become so weakened, it had to investigate and develop any potential military advantage. Increasing the tactical mobility of the troops and employing mobility on the battlefield itself seemed obvious avenues of inquiry. As he examined the theoretical concept of using motorized transport to maneuver infantry on the battlefield, Guderian's thoughts turned to the need to protect motor infantry from hostile enemy fire and from there, naturally, to the tank. [20]

To learn more about the potential of armor Guderian contacted Lieutenant Ernst von Volckheim, a World War I tank commander then studying the use of armor in other armies. Volckheim introduced Guderian to the existing literature on the topic.[21] During the 1920s Guderian read the works of some of the leading European armored warfare theorists of the time and eagerly examined reports of British exercises with mechanized forces. He also wrote some articles for military journals, particularly *Military Weekly*, although he was actually much less prolific than other German armor theorists such as von Volckheim, von Kuhl, and von Vollard-Bockelberg.[22] Between 1922 and 1928 Guderian published only five articles under his own name in *Military Weekly*, and most of these were on mundane and obscure topics.[23] Volckheim—who received a one-sentence mention in Guderian's memoirs—was far more prolific with five books and more than twenty articles. Volckheim was a much more widely recognized proponent of German armored warfare than Guderian throughout the 1920s.[24] Guderian's publications did, however, increase his visibility within the German military, but this was more because he addressed the controversial topic of how and why Germany had lost the Great War rather than because of his ideas on armored warfare, which echoed the theories of other pioneering proponents at the time, particularly von Volckheim.[25]

Guderian tackled the motorization issue with his usual zealous inventiveness. He developed a reputation for clarity of exposition on the controversial topic of the causes of Germany's defeat in the Great War.[26] One of the solutions he advocated was the conversion of what he saw as "archaic" cavalry divisions into mechanized formations, a proposition that understandably alarmed cavalry officers. In these early writings Guderian demonstrated his vision, his impulsive innovation, and his impatient lack of tact.

Too weak to defend itself against its enemies, the *Reichswehr* was psychologically motivated to do things that other armies were not—to seek every advantage and to innovate.[27] Thus it resumed annual maneuvers as early as 1922 and from 1923 began holding exercises with hypothetical and improvised motorized forces. The *Reichswehr* did not look to Guderian's lead in these efforts. However, the Motor Transport Command did have Guderian evaluate these exercises on its behalf, as many other specialist officers did for their respective commands.

Undoubtedly Guderian was a skilled and persuasive proponent—both in writing and vocally—of mechanization. And his dynamic optimism made people remember him. It was thus predictable that in 1924 he was selected to serve on the staff of the 2d Infantry Division (now lead, coincidentally, by his old commander, Tschischwitz) at Stettin as an instructor of military history and tactics. In Stettin Guderian focused on previous German (and other) military failures to justify innovation. His direct, pointed, witty lectures appealed to his students. There is no doubt that he was a dynamic and enthusiastic public speaker, though he was not quite as effective an instructor. His impatience, the considerable demands he made on his students, and his biting sarcasm alienated many of his students, particularly the weaker ones. However, Guderian's personality was polarizing; thus, although it immensely irritated some students, it appealed to others.

Teaching military history stimulated Guderian's creative thoughts and scholarship, as teaching should do for any genuine scholar. He won converts in his classes to his progressive ideas as he increasingly argued that armor could restore "dynamic punch" to the battlefield more than any other weapon.[28] One can see a natural progression in his thought process in his teaching; his lectures gradually shifted focus from conventional military history to advocacy of mechanization. Nevertheless, although he maintained his contacts with the Inspectorate of Transport Troops, Guderian played no direct role in either the secret testing of tanks in Russia or in the procurement of

Germany's first tanks—camouflaged under the innocuous cover name of "tractors" in the mid-1920s.

In January 1927 Guderian was finally promoted to major (advancement was inevitably slow in the small *Reichswehr* officer corps) and in October he received a posting to the Transport Section of the Operations Department of the *Truppenamt*, actually a disguised General Staff. His new mission was to assist in the development of truckborne infantry forces. He dealt with more senior and conservative staff officers—products of an entrenched institutional culture—who saw only the increased tactical mobility that motorization would bring. Guderian continued to develop and to articulate his vision of the strategic use of mechanized forces (but mainly armor) on future battlefields. He clashed repeatedly with the limited vision of the successor to General Tschischwitz—Colonel von Natzer—who saw a more traditional support role for the motor troops in the future. In a small *Reichswehr* with limited resources there were strong reasons for promoting a conventional mission that was much more likely to attract funding than a radical and utterly untested theory held by a few ardent junior-ranked armor enthusiasts.

During the fall of 1928 Guderian was appointed to found a new tactical instruction department within the Transport Section of the Operations Department. It was testimony to the backwardness of the German army that Guderian was one of its leading speakers on tanks but had never stepped foot inside of one![29] Not until he traveled to Sweden in the summer of 1929 did Guderian see his first tank, and he briefly drove a Swedish M21. In his memoirs Guderian exaggerated the significance of this event in the evolution of his ideas on armored warfare, disingenuously suggesting that his experience in Sweden led him that year to the concept of a combined-arms armored division.[30] Yet the notion of combined-arms warfare was hardly novel to German officers of his day: it had been one of the central pillars of the von Seeckt reforms of the 1920s.[31] This was an example of Guderian's tendency to take personal credit for something that was part of a much larger institutional evolution of the interwar German armed forces.

Meanwhile, his former battalion commander was quietly at work bringing the vision he shared with Guderian closer to reality. Lutz, contrary to the impression Guderian offered in his memoirs, was in fact a German armored warfare pioneer in his own right. Lutz enthusiastically and vigorously promoted the study of armor. Even as a section chief in the Weapons Office in 1924–7, Lutz began training his staff in concepts of armored warfare.[32] It was Lutz who insisted that armored tactics be included in the motor transport technical course at Berlin-Moabit. In 1925 his staff studied use of artillery tractors and semitracked vehicles in the Great War. By 1926—five years before Guderian had ever seen a tank—Lutz had concluded that Germany needed both a heavy battle tank and a light exploitation tank. It was Lutz's ideas rather than Guderian's that shaped Germany's first tank programs in the late 1920s.[33]

Equally important was Lutz's predecessor as Inspector General of Motor Transport Troops from 1926–31, Colonel Alfred von Vollard-Bockelberg. In the last three years of the 1920s all seven of Vollard-Bockelberg's motor transport battalions conducted field maneuvers with embryonic mechanized forces comprising dummy tanks, dummy antitank guns, armored cars, and the first prototype tanks.[34] He also advocated a combat role for "motor transport troops."[35] Astonishingly, in his memoirs Guderian failed to make any mention of this important armored warfare pioneer.

That veteran Great War tankers—such as Volckheim and Captain Theofehrn—were seconded to the Motor Transport Troops Inspectorate in the mid-1920s demonstrates that the *Reichswehr* already intended to develop some kind of tank force within the motor transport troops and that Guderian was simply one player—and a junior one at that—on this team of panzer pioneers.[36] As the 1930s arrived, however, new horizons would open for Guderian that would destine him for much bigger things.

Guderian and the 1930s Evolution of German Armor

HISTORIANS HAVE often credited Guderian with the central role in the evolution of German armored forces in the 1930s. This perspective rests heavily on Guderian's own exaggerated self-portrait depicted in his memoirs. While Guderian undoubtedly played an important role in the development of both the panzer division concept and a doctrine of mechanized offensive maneuver warfare, his role was less central than he himself claimed. Repeatedly in his memoirs, Guderian took personal credit for what were, in reality, team accomplishments. In fact, it was the endeavors of a group of officers—including Guderian—that forged the German armored force that helped Germany establish a continental European hegemony during the initial stages of the Second World War.

In 1930 the future German armored force was still an embryo. Germany's first—and ineffective—tank designs were being secretly tested in the Soviet Union, and the *Reichswehr* had embarked on field maneuvers with improvised mechanized forces to examine the theoretical basis of future strategic mechanized maneuver warfare.[1] In the early 1930s, the Germans also began to develop guidelines for the future employment of armored forces based on a logical combination of existing British doctrine, traditional Prussian military tenets, and the military experiences of the Great War.[2] As noted earlier, Guderian's role in these efforts was small. Rather, starting in February 1930, he found himself preoccupied with the daily administrative duties associated with commanding the 3d Motor Transport Battalion. In October 1931 the newly promoted Lieutenant-Colonel Guderian became chief of staff of the Motor Transport Troops Inspectorate.[3] It was not until the summer of 1932 that Guderian participated in divisional field maneuvers that incorporated a combined-arms motorized battle group. This experimental field force, which was the evolutionary product of a concept of armored formation that had been discussed throughout the 1920s both within the *Reichswehr* and the international military journals, was the progenitor of the future panzer division.[4]

In 1931 General Oswald Lutz became the Inspector of Motor Transport Troops. Lutz played a much greater role in the evolution of the German panzer force in the 1930s than Guderian gave him credit for in his memoirs. Lutz received praise from Guderian but only for alleged subordination to Guderian's supposed "leadership." The impression Guderian gave could not be further from the truth. While undoubtedly less visible, Lutz nevertheless was half of a Guderian-Lutz partnership, playing a role that Guderian, with his temperament and lack of seniority, could never have played. Although less extroverted, articulate, and overtly passionate than Guderian, Lutz worked diligently behind the scenes to advance armored warfare theory. Yet Guderian in his memoirs denigrated Lutz's role. Lutz provided a valuable counterbalance for the more excitable, tempestuous, and impatient Guderian, but he also was an accomplished organizer and an articulate, progressive thinker in his own right.[5] In fact, the central tenets of armored warfare that Guderian consistently articulated throughout the 1930s—independence, mass, and surprise—were those previously developed by Lutz.[6] For example, it was Lutz, not Guderian, who wrote the first German doctrinal statements on mechanized warfare.[7]

Most important, Lutz had the authority that Guderian lacked and therefore had greater institutional influence. Lutz's tact allowed him to quietly smooth the feathers that Guderian's abrasive personality so frequently ruffled. Through unobtrusive negotiation and persuasion

Lutz paved the way for Guderian's accomplishments. That Lutz shrewdly pushed Guderian through important command assignments clearly indicates Lutz's leadership role. In early 1930 it was Lutz who gathered dummy tanks and antitank guns, as well as the first new armored cars under Guderian's command in the 3d Motor Transport Battalion, to create Germany's first, permanently constituted, combined-arms mechanized unit. In fact, it is not difficult to conclude that Lutz's role was more important than Guderian's. Moreover, Guderian exaggerated the central role his 3d Motor Transport Battalion played in the evolution of German armored warfare concepts. All seven motor transport battalions were actively engaged, and other units, particularly the 6th and 7th, were involved earlier and more extensively in doctrinal development than Guderian's unit.[8]

The early exercises taught both Lutz and Guderian the need for having an autonomous armored command to control independent armored formations. They also illuminated the enormous problems of tactically controlling armored forces. The seemingly obvious solution was radio communications, which was still in its infancy. Yet, for mechanized forces to conduct successful deep penetration operations—the cornerstone of their strategic capability, as Guderian saw it—both higher headquarters and field commanders had to keep in touch with fast-moving armored forces. There is no doubt that Guderian, the Great War communications officer, instinctively understood the importance of radios for future mechanized warfare and tirelessly lobbied to furnish every future tank with a radio.[9] Yet his efforts occurred within the context of a *Reichswehr* that had extensively discussed the communications needs of future mobile operations and had already come to appreciate by 1932 the central future role the radio would play.[10] Furnishing every tank was an enormous undertaking that would take years to accomplish but that ultimately provided Germany with an operational and tactical edge.

While Guderian's 3d Motor Transport Battalion became the kernel of the future armored force, it was by no means Germany's first combined-arms mechanized unit, as we have already discussed. The ambitious Guderian was less of a team player than Lutz and was determined to be the lead figure. It was fortunate for their symbiotic relationship that Lutz was prepared to remain outside the public glare, working behind the scenes while Guderian took on the public role of advocacy.

As greater resources began to flow to the Motor Transport Inspectorate in the early 1930s, the infantry and cavalry arms showed increasing interest in acquiring some armored vehicles. Lutz's quiet negotiations played an important role in dissipating the institutional challenges this posed for the Inspectorate. At a time when the traditional branches were struggling to define clear institutional roles for themselves in future warfare that would preserve and hopefully expand their resource allocations, "turf" wars were inevitable. In 1932, in order to preserve its primary combat role of operational deep penetration and strategic reconnaissance, the cavalry relinquished the secondary role of tactical reconnaissance to the Motor Transport Command.[11] This allowed the Lutz-Guderian team to acquire the new armored cars then coming into production. Poorly armed and poorly armored, with inadequate cross-country mobility, these cars clearly had no strategic potential in long-range cavalry operations, and the cavalry therefore was prepared to relinquish them to Lutz's command. It is unimaginable that Lutz and Guderian could have wrested control of tactical reconnaissance (and with it armored cars) from the much more powerful cavalry arm had the cavalry not been willing to concede what it considered to be the implausibility of any mission that would rely on them.

This internal institutional wrangling took place against a backdrop of enormous upheaval in Germany. The Great Depression had brought untold socioeconomic misery to Germany, polarizing politics and ruining the credibility of the "alien" Weimar Republic. Out of this turmoil the Nazi Party violently rose to power. In contrast to his behavior in 1919, Guderian initially remained apolitical in the Prussian tradition. Yet many of his former *Freikorps* comrades, with some of whom he still kept in contact, had already gravitated to the Nazi Party and its SA (*Sturm Abteilung*) paramilitary organization, noted for its brutish thuggery. Ideologically Guderian was a nationalist-monarchist: he preferred military commanders to be national political leaders and wholeheartedly supported Paul von Hindenburg as president.

In the 1920s, Guderian had seen little to attract him to what was a radical, fringe right-wing party, one amid many obscure parties.

He apparently expressed no opinion when the Weimar Republic banned Nazis from entering the army in 1927 nor complained about the strong anti-Nazi sentiments widely expressed in the *Reichswehr* in the late 1920s. Indeed, at heart, Guderian was a traditionalist who revered the departed House of Hohenzollern. As a nationalist, he favored strong, authoritarian, centralized right-wing government, and he thought the Nazi Party had the potential to build such a government. More importantly, Guderian held deep anticommunist convictions, which the Nazis also held. He certainly was no Republican or constitutionalist democrat and his faith in the Weimar government was superficial. Yet he remained loyal to Weimar, like so many other Germans, as long as it maintained stability, order, and prosperity. When it failed to rescue Germany from the Great Depression and was swept away by the Nazi rise to power, Guderian did not lament its passing.[12]

Guderian longed for the emergence of another Bismarck to save Germany and restore its national pride and dignity, rebuild and heal the nation, and, most importantly, restore the army to its former social and political preeminence.[13] The Nazis' promise of military rearmament and expansion, as well as their pervasive nationalist and patriotic appeals, won over many in the army, including Guderian.

There can be little doubt that Guderian was gradually won over to supporting National Socialism. Initially, he opposed Hitler and the Nazis. But the threat that communism posed—the Communist Party was, after all, the only viable alternative to the Nazis if Germany's dire domestic problems were to be solved—pushed Guderian toward the Nazis. Guderian saw in Hitler a strong national leader who nonetheless could be controlled by the military. Guderian approved the appointment of Nazi sympathizers to senior positions in the defense establishment after Hitler came to power in January 1933. Clearly, Guderian hoped that the new political leadership would prove more receptive to his ideas. Events would prove his hunch to be correct; but he naively continued to believe that the army could control Hitler from behind the scenes as it had often manipulated Weimar leaders before.

It seems clear, therefore, that Guderian's political position regarding the Nazis changed. We can also conclude that he changed his position largely for pragmatic reasons. He came to see that the Nazis were best for the country and for the army—and, conveniently, for his own substantial ambitions. However, in a practical sense, Guderian also found it necessary to mentally dissociate Hitler from Nazi party violence. This willful ignoring of reality allowed Guderian to retain enormous faith in Hitler as the strong national leadership figure he craved, while turning a blind eye to the violence, anti-Semitism, and persecution unleashed at Hitler's bidding.

Though there is nothing in Guderian's writings to suggest that he was an anti-Semite, as an occasionally practicing Lutheran he shared the widespread ambivalence toward Jews and Judaism that characterized Christian Europe. He certainly displayed no sympathy for the plight of German, and later, European Jewry under the genocidal persecution that Hitler and the Nazis would unleash on Europe.

Guderian hoped the Nazis would create his dreamed-of panzer force, and certainly the Nazi leadership generally exhibited progressive attitudes toward automobiles (they did introduce the Volkswagen—the "people's car") and were committed to military expansion and innovation. His desire to see an independent armored force restore Germany's national pride and bring military honor to Guderian himself thus bound him to national socialism. His enthusiasm and support were conditioned by ambition, greed, and a desire for military glory. Guderian's political naiveté allowed him, like so many Germans, foolishly to see only the benefit in Hitler.

Lieutenant-General Lutz and his chief of staff, Colonel Guderian, worked tirelessly together while the Nazis consolidated their power. Lutz formed Germany's first tank training company at Zossen on 1 November 1933.[14] Early in 1934, the ambitious Guderian obtained an opportunity to demonstrate personally for Hitler in embryo a future panzer division (which included the brand new Panzer I training tank). It has been alleged that at the conclusion of the demonstration Hitler said, "That is what I need," fueling Guderian's hopes.[15] Yet, precisely what Hitler may have meant by these words is not clear. It is possible that Hitler saw the emerging panzer forces as an excellent propaganda tool, completing the image of Nazi modernity and military preparedness that in fact masked profound weakness, but which gave Germany leverage over its neighbors as Hitler cautiously embarked on aggressive foreign policy initiatives, such as the repudiation of the Treaty of Versailles in 1935, that buttressed his domestic popularity.[16] Certainly, Hitler continued to give the new Luftwaffe priority and did not afford the panzer forces any special priority in rearmament. In fact, he bound the entire German military to himself by allowing dramatic expansion of all branches of service and all arms within the army with minimal oversight and no clear strategic direction.[17]

An offensive-oriented armored force simply would not have fulfilled the national security requirements of Germany in the mid-1930s when the primary task for the army remained defense against neighbors—Poland, France, and Czechoslovakia—which were ill-disposed toward both Germany and its Nazi leadership. Thus, during the early 1930s even Guderian couched the need for a panzer force in predominantly defensive terms. As a Prussian, Guderian was particularly concerned about the Polish threat and therefore, like many senior German officers of his day, conceived of mobile forces harassing and disrupting an invading enemy by attacking its flanks and rear using greater mobility.[18] Though he did envision the possibility of armored forces achieving a breakthrough in their own right, he thought of this as a secondary role to the primary mission of national defense. In this regard, Guderian was no innovator; he simply embraced the prevailing views regarding national defense and military doctrine that had evolved in the *Reichswehr* during the 1920s.[19]

As he encountered mounting opposition within the army to his radical, ambitious plans, Guderian consciously reached out to the Nazi Party leadership in search of influential allies. For example, he cultivated a relationship with National Socialist Motor Corps (NSKK) leader Adolf Hühnlein: the NSKK was a party auxiliary force that manifested the party's modernity and commitment to motor transport. It was Hühnlein who took Guderian to his first Nazi Party meeting in 1933 and worked with Guderian to train tank drivers in NSKK motor transport schools.[20] Guderian's determination to curry favor with senior Nazi leaders, essentially for his own self-interest, contributed to the widespread perception that soon emerged among his fellow officers that Guderian was a "Nazi" officer.[21] Despite his efforts to curry favor, Germany's first field maneuvers with an experimental panzer division, conducted at Münsterlager in August

1935, were led by Lieutenant-General Maximilian Freiherr von Weichs, a senior cavalry commander committed to mechanization.[22]

In his memoirs Guderian simplistically caricatured the opposition he faced as a struggle between progressive reformers and the reactionary conservatism of the army high command (the *Oberkommando des Heeres*, or OKH), its General Staff, the infantry and artillery.[23] Yet, the reality was much more complex. Guderian falsely labeled General Beck, the army chief of staff, as a conservative opponent of mechanization.[24] In reality, Beck sought the army's holistic offensive enhancement and he feared that Guderian's insistent demands for resources threatened such balanced development.[25] The infantry and artillery were rightly fearful of the institutional threat that the new mobile troops command constituted and dug in their heels in defense of their respective arms. They demanded compelling evidence that the new mechanized forces would not only be successful but represented the most cost-effective use of scarce military resources before taking the leap of faith of diverting massive resources to them. Such investment could not be subsequently recouped in a time of fiscal constraint, if Guderian's claims proved illusory. In fact, one historian has concluded that Guderian's claim to have had a "long, drawn-out fight" with Beck was "sheer exaggeration."[26] In reality, in many respects, Beck was more progressive than Guderian: Beck fully endorsed the idea of a panzer division and its future strategic use, and he favored equipping it with the heavier Panzer III and IV tanks, whereas Guderian, committed to mass and mobility, preferred to equip them rapidly with large numbers of the light Panzer I training tank.[27]

The "progressives" versus "reactionaries" dichotomy presented in *Panzer Leader* was typical of the simplistic way in which Guderian viewed these institutional struggles. Yet, Guderian caricatured his opponents inaccurately and his dismissive attitudes toward their tendency to look out for their own interests not only reflected his naiveté but also hampered the evolution of the armored force. Within the cavalry, for example, there were many younger officers who eagerly embraced mechanization as providing future institutional relevance for the service. But Guderian's uncompromising thirst for a completely autonomous armored force, without any willingness to share it, provoked opposition and resistance.

It was Guderian's antipathy toward the cavalry, much more than any reactionary tendencies on its part, that hampered cooperation between the mobile troops command and Germany's mounted soldiers. For a strong impetus toward innovation existed among the cavalry as the branch searched for continuing institutional relevance. In fact, several of Germany's most successful wartime panzer commanders—Ewald von Kleist, Eberhard von Mackensen, and Freiherr Geyr von Schweppenburg, for example—had been interwar cavalry officers.[28] Guderian's disdain for the cavalry seems to have stemmed from negative experiences he had while serving with the I Cavalry Corps during the failed Schlieffen Plan offensive during the late summer of 1914 and again at Verdun in 1916. Then, during the 1920s, Guderian came to view the cavalry as anachronistic. Not only were his views on the subject absolute, but his inability to disguise his contempt when dealing with senior cavalry officers accentuated the friction that his dogmatic opinions created. Guderian's disdain of the cavalry was so extreme that he consistently opposed the integration of "archaic" cavalry personnel into the new mobile troops command, even though logic dictated this course of action. At a time when the fledgling combat branch needed all the resources it could acquire, Guderian's antipathy toward the cavalry led him to reject a substantial injection of personnel and resources.

Instead, Guderian held to a Utopian desire for a completely "new" branch untainted by any of the traditions and prejudices of the existing arms. This was an absurd notion: military institutions do not engender new combat arms out of thin air; it was inevitable that a substantial proportion of the manpower and resources for the mobile troops command would come from the cavalry. Moreover, cavalry formations had formed the bulk of the experimental motorized and mechanized forces activated during the early 1930s.[29] For example, the cavalry had already played an important role in the 1934 annual exercises in which the 3d Cavalry Division had been partially mechanized to test mobile operations.[30] Because of Guderian's antipathy and insistence on absolute control of anything connected to mechanization, however, institutional cooperation derailed during the 1930s.

In the late 1930s opposition emerged between the pioneers of armored warfare and the artillery, as the latter came to fear Guderian's all-grasping encroachment on traditional gunner preserves. Again, biographers have usually accepted Guderian's distorted adversarial depiction of this turf war. Yet, again, the reality was more complex. Macksey's claim that Guderian first envisioned self-propelled artillery in 1934, but that the gunners "bitterly opposed self-propelled artillery until the outbreak of war" because they "did not believe in fast-moving combat" is erroneous.[31] The artillery was actually progressive: it had developed several improvised self-propelled guns late in the Great War and several experimental self-propelled guns mounted on agricultural tractors during the 1920s, all without Guderian's assistance.[32] The gunners had also extensively discussed the impact of mechanization on artillery operations and explored the possibilities of mechanizing artillery. Yet, like the bulk of the German army, they saw conventional methods of artillery fighting continuing in the near future. The technology—particularly command and control—that would have been required to realize Guderian's vision simply did not exist in the 1930s. Despite these limitations, the artillery committed an experimental motorized battalion to field maneuvers as early as 1932 and had a self-propelled artillery battalion establishment slated into the first planned panzer division organization.[33]

Again the obstacle was competitiveness on Guderian's part rather than conservative opposition to change on the artillery's part. Guderian demanded that the artillery create new weapon systems from its own very limited resources and then hand over these weapons, and the important artillery role that came with it, to a brand new arm, without any combat experience, and that was based exclusively on an as-yet untested theory propounded by an aggressive maverick innovator. This was the meat of the gunners' objections and the impatient Guderian proved even less successful in this acrimonious struggle with the gunners than he had with the cavalry. Moreover, the artillery had friends in powerful places. Wilhelm Keitel, Jodl, Warlimont, Beck, and Halder—leading figures in the German military of the 1930s—were all career gunners. These senior commanders had Hitler's ear and successfully defended gunner interests against Guderian's ardent demands.

Lieutenant-General Lutz headed the new independent Mobile Troops Command that materialized in July 1934 and Guderian, now a colonel, became his chief of staff. But the Panzer I training tank held limited promise and certainly did little to dispel the healthy skepticism of many senior officers. Small, weak, poorly armed and armored, and with limited cross-country performance, Germany's first tank—the Panzer I—was utterly incapable of realizing the strategic potential Guderian claimed armored forces could have. But it was all that a brand-new German tank industry could initially produce.[34]

During August 1934 an embryonic armored division drawn from units of the Mobile Troops Command demonstrated the potential of mechanized forces. The next step was the formation of Germany's first three panzer divisions, which emerged in October 1935. At a time when Germany only had twenty-nine divisions, this represented an enormous diversion of resources into an as yet unproven arm.[35] It is unthinkable that three armored divisions could have emerged if Beck and the traditional arms were as hostile to armor as Guderian claimed. Again, whatever hostility Beck felt must have derived from Guderian's hotheaded impetuosity rather than from opposition to armored warfare concepts as Beck sought the balanced development of mechanization along paths consistent with perceived German national security requirements.[36] Equally revealing is that senior cavalry officers commanded two of these three panzer divisions.[37]

Beck appointed Colonel Guderian to command the 2d Panzer Division. This is not what Guderian wanted and one has to suspect that the appointment was intended by Beck to distract Guderian from policy-advocacy with the requirements of field command. Perhaps Beck hoped that actual command of a panzer division would temper some of Guderian's more fanciful demands. But committed to balance and far better attuned with the imperatives of institutional harmony, Beck went on to form a panzer brigade for infantry support (and later another), in opposition to Guderian's plans. Inevitably, as the Mobile Troops Command grew, it invited grasping hands.

Many senior officers—field and General Staff alike—remained doubtful of the claims made by the armor advocates. It was Lutz more than Guderian who transformed the Mobile Troops Command into a strong, coherent branch in the late 1930s. Quietly, with much less fuss and rancor than Guderian was raising, Lutz negotiated, cajoled, listened, and compromised to push forward his command more effectively than Guderian could ever have done.

Another major issue that the German army had to tackle was the transportation of motorized infantry. At hand were two-wheel-drive trucks of minimal cross-country capability. When these failed in a 1937 exercise, Guderian once again demonstrated his impatient, arrogant egoism and impudence by storming up to Army commander-in-chief Fritsch and bitterly lambasting the inadequacy of these vehicles and the refusal of senior commanders to pay heed to Guderian's previous condemnation of the trucks' deficiencies.

Guderian's grandiose demands also hampered the panzer division concept. The first panzer division establishment Lutz and Guderian formulated in August 1935 required no less than 481 tanks plus armored personnel carriers, which did not exist even as a design concept.[38] Yet, Guderian was happy with the Panzer I light tanks because throughout the 1930s he retained enormous faith in the tactical and operational advantage of maneuver. He believed that mobility would be the most important quality of a successful tank force and therefore dismissed the limitations of machine gun-only armament and armor that offered protection against small arms fire. It was only during 1936 that he began to warm to the idea of a heavier tank of up to 70 tons with an armor-penetrating gun, intended to "assault permanent fortifications"—something utterly beyond the capabilities of German industry. He had to settle for something less—the result was the Panzer IV tank, a design concept long supported by both Beck and Lutz.

During 1935 there emerged a stopgap Panzer II light reconnaissance tank and the Panzer IV medium tank in a direct support role armed with a short-barreled 75mm gun with poor armor penetration. These two tanks were both lightly armored and unable to withstand direct hits from existing enemy antitank or artillery rounds. Because Guderian believed that tanks would have to fight tanks (though he had never personally witnessed a tank engagement), the Panzer III battle tank also evolved during 1935 as a dedicated tank killer. From the beginning Guderian wanted this tank armed with a potent 50mm gun, but technical limitations (no such gun existed) forced him to initially accept a 37mm gun. The key design feature of the Panzer III and IV, however, was their ability to have their armament and armor enhanced in the future.

But the selfish Guderian, obsessed with advancing the interests of the panzer force at any cost, never considered what was good for the army as a whole. Thus he bitterly opposed Beck's more prudent desire to generate mechanization more broadly through the army. When the infantry demanded motorized transport to pull their new, hitherto horse-drawn antitank guns and infantry guns (a valuable Beck innovation), Guderian bitterly opposed this "loss" of resources, even though the increased mobile firepower this brought to the infantry certainly increased its effectiveness, allowing it to play an important role in the Blitzkrieg successes, Guderian's claims to the contrary notwithstanding.[39] Again the egotistical Guderian believed that his mechanized forces could win wars unaided, but events would prove he was wrong. The intimate coordination of mechanized forces with artillery, infantry, and engineers as well as tactical aviation proved to be the key to the Blitzkrieg successes of the early years of the Second World War. The reality of mobile operations therefore proved to be quite different from Guderian's prewar vision.

In 1935–8 Guderian bitterly opposed the new artillery assault gun concept (an artillery howitzer mounted in an armored superstructure on a modified Panzer III tank chassis) designed to augment the mobile firepower available to the infantry. In his memoirs he blamed gunner conservatism for ensuring that only five prototype assault guns existed when Germany went to war in 1939.[40] The truth is that the assault gun concept had the full backing of the gunners and had never been Guderian's idea.[41] Gunner progressivism had indeed ensured that a fully self-propelled artillery battalion was incorporated into the first plans for a panzer division in August 1935, but it disappeared for future tables of organization as the controversy over control of self-propelled artillery escalated.[42] In fact, it was Beck, Guderian's nemesis, whose concern both for balance and for restoring the offensive power of the infantry saw him back the gunners and promote the assault gun concept in the mid-1930s despite Guderian's resistance.[43] Again, Guderian narrow-mindedly saw the assault gun as diverting precious resources—the chassis of the Panzer III tank—from his armored force. Yet the *Sturmgeschütz* assault gun that the artillery developed ultimately proved to be one of the very best German armored fighting vehicles of the Second World War. Its capacity for upgrading in armor and armament in the middle of conflict made it the most numerous, cost effective, and efficient German tank killer of the war. Guderian's prejudices ensured that he completely failed to appreciate the value of this weapon for far too long.

Much to Guderian's chagrin, reconnaissance units also returned to the command of the cavalry during this period. This move actually made sense, because reconnaissance had been the central mission of cavalry since time immemorial and because the army continued to foresee the use of light mechanized forces more mobile than Guderian's tank-heavy panzer divisions. Motorized infantry units similarly (and rightly) remained in the hands of the infantry who raised four motorized infantry divisions. Though Guderian denigrated this initiative, too, it was both logical and necessary because, as Beck and others rightly saw, infantry had to be able to keep up with fast-moving mechanized forces to assist them in future mobile warfare. Subsequently, three (later four) light mechanized divisions were formed, with a smaller tank establishment, to conduct operational reconnaissance and deep-penetration operations traditionally performed by cavalry. Guderian falsely claimed that these new divisions were created to placate the powerful cavalry arm. In reality, light mechanized divisions were widely deemed necessary within the army because Guderian's first panzer divisions were so "heavy" and required such substantial logistic support that real doubts remained about their operational mobility. These doubts were confirmed during the 1938 Austrian *Anschluss* (annexation) and in field exercises in the late 1930s.[44] The light divisions were viewed to be more self-sustaining and capable of fast, deep exploitation of a penetration achieved by the panzer divisions. They were thus doctrinally viewed as a complement to, rather than as a rival for, the panzer divisions, as Guderian saw them.

The most important accomplishment effected by the prewar German armored warfare pioneers was the 1938 formation of the world's first corps-level command for mechanized forces, the XVI Motorized Corps, which took command of all three armored divisions and was subordinated to the Fourth Group Command along with new corps to command the light mechanized divisions and motorized infantry divisions, respectively. This represented the creation of the world's first mechanized command capable of independent strategic operations. Yet it was Colonel-General von Brauchtisch, a senior field commander who had organized Germany's earliest mechanized exercises in 1923, not Guderian, who commanded the group.

Guderian fully embraced Hitler's plan to press ahead with territorial changes in Europe. Even though the German military was not yet ready for war, Hitler would use the threat of war, and even short limited mobile operations if necessary, to achieve his political goals. By 1937 Guderian's thinking had shifted—in line with Hitler's increasingly aggressive foreign policy—to the offensive employment of the panzer force.

During the fall of 1936, Lutz suggested that Guderian write *Achtung! Panzer!* as a polemical promotion of the Mobile Troops Command and its concept of independent strategic mechanized operations. Guderian produced a rush job—an idiosyncratic assemblage of some of his war academy lectures and a potted review of military history that relied heavily on the ideas of other German armored warfare theorists, particularly Ludwig Ritter von Eimannsberger.[45] Lutz probably asked Guderian to write *Achtung! Panzer!* because he accurately discerned both the mounting opposition to the panzer arm and the outstretching of inviting hands. Again it is interesting that Lutz was the instigator of this work, which, despite its limitations, became a best seller. Guderian probably also had the additional motive of flattering and currying favor with Hitler. Guderian was still too lowly to move in Hitler's circles; it was not until August 1936 that he was promoted to major general.

In any discussion of the differences of opinion regarding the development of armored forces, it is important to remember that many of the criticisms of the anti-armor exponents made sense. The fundamental strategic objection to mechanization was Germany's weak strategic position and its limited natural source of oil and its derivatives, which left the German war economy dependent on foreign imports that might be threatened in time of war.[46] Both Hitler and Guderian ignored these fundamental strategic realities: as kindred

Social Darwinists, they shared the belief that only the strong would survive, that Germany was a strong nation, and that force was the ultimate arbiter of international relations. Guderian thus embraced Hitler's aggressive foreign policy.

But Guderian was disturbed by Hitler's purging of Fritsch (on trumped-up charges) and Blomberg, with the attendant diminution of the honor and prestige of the armed forces that Guderian held dear. This demonstrated that Guderian was not yet completely in Hitler's camp nor yet completely suffused by national socialism. But Guderian expressed pleasure at the resultant personnel shuffle that made Wilhelm Keitel chief of the Armed Forces High Command (*Oberkommando der Wehrmacht*, or OKW), Brauchitsch the army commander-in-chief, and Reichenau the commander of the Fourth Group Command and, thus, Guderian's new commanding officer. Guderian's in-laws, the Keitels, and Wilhelm Keitel's promotion, also gave Guderian access to the senior military hierarchy and to new channels to reach the Führer as he earnestly sought to do. During this command shuffle Guderian also received a promotion to lieutenant general and was put in charge of the XVI Corps, which commanded all three armored divisions—as his former superior, Lutz, found himself among those purged. The politically naive Guderian failed to discern Hitler's ulterior motives as he ousted the senior military leaders and took the military in a vice-like grip. Indeed, in the practice of Machiavellian politics Guderian remained a neophyte, and his yearning for a strong national leader blinded him to Hitler's deficiencies. Still, in his memoirs Guderian claimed that he was demoralized and dismayed by the departure of Fritsch and Blomberg.[47]

General Lutz's forced retirement in 1938 illuminated the powerful institutional forces now arrayed against the upstart Mobile Troops Command. That these opponents successfully targeted Lutz surely indicates how important a player they perceived him to be in the development of the panzer force. Only in the spring of 1938 would Guderian obtain his first operational experience commanding mechanized forces (albeit one devoid of any actual fighting), when his 2d Panzer Division spearheaded the German annexation of Austria. In his memoirs, while admitting defects in his division's performance, Guderian disingenuously glossed over the myriad deficiencies that marred the first operational employment of a German armored division, and provided an extended "defense" of its performance.[48] It is important to recognize the abysmal performance of the 2d Panzer Division in its unopposed march on Vienna.[49]

On 10 March 1938, Guderian received orders to mobilize his 2d Panzer Division from its peacetime garrison at Würzburg and "annex" Austria two days later. Guderian was thrilled at the prospect of demonstrating the effectiveness of his mechanized forces, despite the minimal advance notice that resulted in a frantic and chaotic mobilization and deployment. His division was instructed to advance 250 miles just to reach the Austrian frontier and then cross it immediately. Moreover, after the division's poor performance in the 1937 maneuvers, Guderian was determined to make sure that his command excelled so as to demonstrate the efficacy of armored forces. The reputation of the Mobile Troops Command was at stake!

Inexperience and lack of planning soon turned the mobilization into chaos.[50] Only parts of the 2d Panzer Division could be made fully operational, and many tanks were unserviceable.[51] Deficient command and control rapidly turned the approach march into anarchy.[52] The division's units became splintered and spread out over several hundred miles—and this was even before they reached the Austrian frontier.[53] Thus on the 12th, only half the division managed to cross the Austrian border at all, and it did so hours behind schedule, without any of its tanks or support services.[54]

But the biggest problems were logistical. Supply services proved woefully ill-prepared and ill-equipped: the division could mobilize just 10 percent of its authorized fuel trucks and widespread, unauthorized "appropriation" of civilian vehicles failed to diminish this shortfall.[55] What is more, divisional quartermasters soon realized that they had woefully underestimated the actual fuel requirements necessary for a panzer division in combat operations. Thus Guderian's spearheads repeatedly ran out of fuel on the roads to Vienna and had to be resupplied from commercial Austrian gasoline stations. Unfortunately Austrian commercial fuel contained less octane, resulting in poor mileage and widespread engine fouling that caused many breakdowns. Consequently, many of Guderian's tanks required a major overhaul on arrival in Vienna.[56] After just two days and without any

Austrian resistance, the division had "lost any semblance of being a combat formation," its after-action report concluded.[57] It was hardly the accomplishment Guderian had sought. Indeed, had it been a contested invasion of a genuinely hostile neighbor, the Austrians could have simply destroyed their gas stations and the 2d Panzer Division would have taken weeks to arrive in Vienna. Indeed, the division itself concluded that any Austrian resistance would have placed the success of the *Anschluss* into jeopardy.[58]

Once in Austria, Guderian developed a friendship with SS *Obergrüppenführer* Sepp Dietrich, an "Old Fighter" who commanded the *Leibstandarte* SS Adolf Hitler, Hitler's bodyguard regiment. Dietrich was a favorite of the Führer and moved within his inner circle. Dietrich admired Guderian's purpose, clarity, and determination. Guderian admired Dietrich because he had been a tank gunner in the Great War and had thus actually fought in a tank, something that Guderian had never done. Because Dietrich was a powerful figure with direct access to the Führer, Guderian carefully cultivated a relationship with him. He would remain on good terms with Dietrich until the end of the war. Guderian used Dietrich's personal relationship to his advantage: on 10 March, Dietrich passed Guderian's suggestion to Hitler that German tanks enter Austria bedecked with Swastikas and German flags to demonstrate their friendly nationalist intent toward the Austrians. Hitler readily accepted. This was the first time Guderian had had a specific influence on Hitler's decision-making. Thereafter Guderian nurtured his friendship with Dietrich for his own self-interest. Though not a Nazi ideologically, Guderian was prepared to cultivate close ties with senior party officials in pursuit of his own goals.[59]

Guderian took part in the charade that passed for a triumphal German military victory parade through Vienna. Guderian stood proudly beside his Führer on the balcony in Linz when Hitler addressed the German and Austrian people. It was undoubtedly the pinnacle of his military career to date. Hitler was willing to accept the charade of a flawless occupation because such an image served his purposes—it inflated German military strength and capabilities in his enemies' eyes—but it is unlikely that he personally was duped.

The German army was less impressed than Guderian. On their return to barracks, the units involved used their usual professional efficiency to write highly critical after-action reports: fuel supply had been woefully deficient, march discipline terrible, and traffic control chaotic. Nevertheless Guderian succeeded in covering up the debacle of the march on Vienna and won official praise and gratitude of the Führer for the performance of mobile troops in the occupation. However, even Guderian admitted to a 30 percent breakdown among his tanks. The actual figure was much higher, as the after-action reports attested.[60] Guderian turned to remedying these deficiencies with his usual vigor and diligence so that they would not embarrass him again in the future. If this had been real combat, Guderian would have been unprepared and assuredly defeated.

As a soldier, Guderian was captivated by the Führer's boldness and his determination to annex Austria, seeing in Hitler the same impetuosity and optimism that were the foundation of Guderian's character. Guderian viewed Hitler as a great man and a natural leader destined to shape the history of the German people, and he therefore gave him his allegiance. He had no inkling of just exactly how disastrously and for how long Hitler would shape that destiny. Yet, Guderian would remain a loyal servant of the Nazi state until the dying days of the Third Reich.

In 1936–9, during the Spanish Civil War, Guderian continued to pursue his cause of building up an armored force. Despite the commitment of a German tank battalion, static warfare characterized much of this complex struggle. Although the war acted as a weapons testing ground for the Germans, it was tactical aviation that emerged from the conflict as the most promising new weapon.[61] The strategic potential that airplanes seemed to possess ensured them publicity and resources. So the Spanish Civil War provided little validation for the self-proclaimed apostle of German armored warfare.

In the last year of peace, Guderian cultivated a personal relationship with Hitler. He received a second visit from Hitler at a field exercise in 1938 and it is certain that he came to the attention of Hitler after Vienna. Indeed, he became a darling of the Führer and began to receive rare invitations to dinner and to attend the opera with him. Consequently, Hitler gave Guderian's XVI Motorized Corps a central role in occupying the Sudetenland. His private correspondence leaves little doubt that Guderian believed Hitler's propaganda that the Sudeten Germans were living under terrible oppression, even though nothing could be further from the truth.[62] Guderian the inveterate nationalist fully approved of Hitler's goals and methods. Hitler's dramatic and bloodless success at Munich in September 1938, when Chamberlain (pursuing a misguided policy of appeasement), gave Hitler the Sudetenland without his having to fire a shot, bound Guderian to the "great leader" he had yearned to see take the helm of the German government.[63] His deliverer had arrived and it would be a long while before Guderian saw through the propaganda and understood that this "great" man would lead Germany to ruin. Even then, he never broke from his oath of loyalty, but rather he feebly sought to minimize what he came to see as Hitler's disastrous military leadership.

During October 1938, Hitler (according to Guderian) apparently discussed with Brauchitsch the idea of appointing Guderian as Chief of Armored Troops to control all motorized troops, including tanks, motor infantry, and mechanized cavalry. This was a sensible initiative that would have given Guderian much greater power. But Guderian initially turned down the position because he thought it lacked sufficient authority. Hitler pushed him to accept the job (the Keitels again acting as intermediaries), and Guderian finally received promotion to General of Armored Troops. However, it was Colonel von Schell, the motorization expert on the General Staff, who was the chief architect of a unified Mobile Troops Command, in what may have been part of an effort to limit Guderian's power.[64]

When Hitler occupied the rump Czechoslovakia in March 1939, Guderian perceived that Hitler had gone too far. His trip to Britain that summer confirmed the dramatic hardening of western opinion against Germany and Hitler, which dramatically increased the prospects of a war that Guderian did not believe Germany was ready for. Guderian thought it inappropriate to annex Czechoslovakia, with its predominantly non-German population. But like a good Prussian officer, he kept his own counsel and greatly appreciated the addition of the large and impressive Czech tank plant to his deficient panzer arm, strengthening it immeasurably on the eve of war.

As the clouds of war approached in the summer of 1939, Guderian expressed opposition to hostilities but not because he believed Nazi aggression to be immoral, nor because it would bring untold death and destruction to the world and risk ruin. Guderian despised the Catholic, Slavic Poles who now occupied parts of his native, beloved Prussia. He thus never expressed any moral objections regarding invading Poland. And like so many other Germans, he ignored the mounting evidence of the regime's growing persecution of German Jews and other "racial undesirables." Guderian opposed Hitler's aggression simply because he did not think his vaunted panzer arm was yet ready for combat.

During 1939 Brauchitsch became fearful of Guderian's rising influence and his deepening friendship with Hitler. In fact, during the last year of peace, the nature of the opposition to Guderian among the military changed. It became less centered on his radical ideas and more on his ambitious, egotistical, impetuous, maverick personality. Guderian thus became a political catalyst, a situation that was primarily his own fault. Incapable of ready compromise in the dispute between panzer and cavalry troops, he failed in his efforts to modernize the cavalry. His opponents struck him a damaging blow—and, likely, a calculated insult—when initial wartime mobilization schedules posted him to command a second-line infantry corps assigned to a defensive mission in the west. Guderian was furious and expended much capital calling in favors and using his Keitel connections to change the assignment. But he only narrowly succeeded and he spent the summer of 1939 fearing that the forces of conservatism had triumphed and he would never regain command of his beloved XVI Corps. He was right: on 22 August 1939—just three days before Hitler's chosen invasion date—Guderian received command of a new, untried XIX Motorized Corps then forming up in Pomerania.

Throughout the late 1930s, Guderian seethed as obstacles hampered his frantic efforts to prepare the armored troops for war. Overweening ambition spurred him on as his opponents threw obstacles in his way. His enormous energy carried him forward as he tried by dint of energy, insolence, and confrontation to knock down roadblock after roadblock thrown in his path. How well he would succeed, only the audit of war would tell.

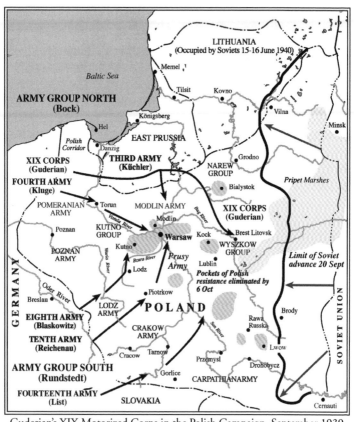

Guerian's XIX Motorized Corps in the Polish Campaign, September 1939

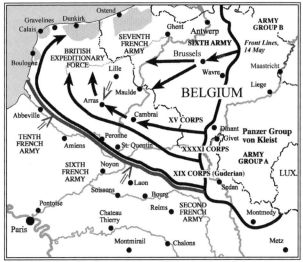

Advance of Guderian's XIX Motorized Corps from the River
Meuse to the English Channel, 13–14 May 1940

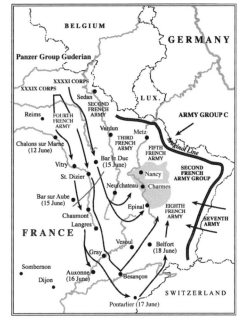

Advance of Panzer Group Guderian from the
River Aisne to the Swiss Frontier, 5–25 June 1940

Guderian Goes to War, 1939–1940

"The Goddess of Battle will crown only the most daring with laurels." [1]

During August 1939 Guderian was busy preparing for major mechanized maneuvers slated for the fall. In the middle of this preparation, on 22 August, his vehement protests against his scheduled wartime command of a reserve infantry corps finally bore fruit as he was ordered to take command of the newly constituted XIX Motorized Corps then forming up in Pomerania. Thus, at very short notice he received command of the northern spearhead of the German invasion of Poland.

In assessing Guderian's role in Germany's dramatic military achievements in 1939 and 1940, it is important to emphasize that Guderian habitually found himself in the right place at the right time. Though he was delighted to be rid of command of an infantry corps in a backwater, the egotistical Guderian was actually disappointed with the role assigned to him for the Polish campaign. For the main intended *Schwerpunkt*, or center of gravity, of the German attack lay in Silesia where Army Group South would advance to the Vistula south of Warsaw. The bulk of German armor—two panzer and two light mechanized divisions—were committed here for an advance through good tank country under Guderian's former command, the XVI Motorized Corps, and he resented not being given the chance to lead the corps he had nurtured. A more senior cavalry commander, General Erich von Hoepner, had received command of the corps, and he aggressively pushed his armor toward Warsaw into the teeth of the deployed Polish field forces.[2]

Guderian's new XIX Corps received a lesser role: to spearhead the advance of the German northern wing across the Polish Corridor to reestablish direct contact with isolated East Prussia, which had been separated from the rest of Germany in the humiliating Versailles settlement of 1919. Afterward, Guderian's corps was to traverse through East Prussia and then turn due south to advance on Warsaw, link up with the spearheads of Army Group South, and envelope the bulk of the Polish forces west of the Vistula in a classic Prussian encirclement-annihilation battle (*Kesselschlacht*).[3] For this more limited mission, Guderian received only 14.5 percent of the German armor committed to the Polish Campaign.[4]

The German leadership made Guderian's thrust the lesser prong because it anticipated less resistance in the Polish Corridor, where defenses were weaker than those in Silesia, and because Guderian would pass through friendly East Prussian territory. Guderian received only one of Germany's six panzer divisions.[5] His corps was reinforced by two motorized infantry divisions, formations whose creation Guderian had vehemently opposed in the late 1930s and which, initially at least in Poland, he clearly regarded as inferior, ancillary forces to his vaunted, if solitary, panzer division.[6] His command was thus a considerable reduction from the concentrated armored force he had dreamed of leading.

At least Guderian would get to "rescue" isolated East Prussia and would be fighting in former West Prussian territory that included his birthplace of Kulm. In keeping with his Prussian heritage, Guderian despised the Poles and therefore articulated no misgivings whatsoever about the blatant German provocations that precipitated war with Poland. Here at last was the audit of war that would prove all his theories, all those hard years of labor worthwhile, while simultaneously resurrecting German rule throughout Prussia. Guderian also fancied himself in the role of a Teutonic Knight of old, liberating his ancestral family estates in Gross-Klonia and Kulm. In fact,

Guderian selfishly deployed the 3d Panzer Division, his spearhead, to allow it to advance directly toward this ancestral estate! At the same time, underappreciating the value of his two motorized divisions, he initially set them tertiary flank missions on unpropitious axes of advance.[7] From the outset Guderian banked heavily on the success of his lone panzer division. As would happen so often in his military career, Guderian gambled and his gamble paid off.

Unfortunately, repeated friendly-fire mishaps and unforeseen checks by Polish rearguards marred Guderian's first day of combat as a panzer field commander. It was fortunate that the Poles his troops encountered were unprepared to make a determined stand. Indeed, the mission of the Polish forces was to fight a delaying defense, while preserving their strength intact for the major battle for the Polish heartland. The Polish government recognized the impossibility of holding the Polish Corridor in the face of a major German invasion and were not inclined to sacrifice forces in pursuit of such a hopeless task.[8]

That reconquest of his family estates was uppermost in Guderian's mind is evident in his reaction to a regimental commander's actions. When this commander halted his first day's advance within sight of Gross-Klonia, Guderian ordered him to press his advance at night, despite the risks. His determination to recapture his ancestral estate at the earliest opportunity led to what even he subsequently admitted were "serious casualties" as he forced the advance during the night and through a dangerous morning fog the next day. The next morning, as the fighting diminished, he moved to the front of the forces to lead personally a triumphant liberation of the ancient family estate.[9] In his memoirs, Guderian failed to mention that once he had "liberated" his ancestral family estate, the Guderian family quietly and quickly evicted its owners and repossessed it.[10]

Guderian proved a human dynamo, leading personally from the front and motivating resumption of the attack. He drove forth his command furiously with the fervor of conviction. He always showed up where the fighting was thickest, where the *Schwerpunkt* was, and accepted great personal risk. The fearless Guderian in his arrogance believed that destiny would protect him from injury. In fact, he had barely escaped becoming a victim of friendly fire on 1 September, when his command vehicle was bracketed by short-falling German artillery rounds and his driver crashed into a ditch frantically trying to escape; Guderian was lucky to escape serious injury. His personal interventions, his fearlessness, and his public, humiliating dressing-down of subordinate commanders who sparked his ire won him the acclaim of his troops. Yet, these same attributes simultaneously earned him the enmity of many a senior officer whose command prerogatives Guderian carelessly and thoughtlessly trampled over. For instance, Guderian soon found himself at odds with the 3d Panzer Division commander—Freiherr Geyr von Schweppenburg—another future rising star of the armored force.

Other problems bedeviled Guderian's first field command. From the beginning, logistic deficiencies plagued his advance, despite all the prewar preparations. His attack temporarily stalled on the second day of the invasion as the vanguard ran out of fuel. This occurred because of the furious pace with which Guderian drove his spearheads forward; he believed that mobility provided a crucial operational advantage, and by inclination he always preferred to be on the move forward. By 5 September, the XIX Corps had penetrated across the Polish Corridor and linked up with forces advancing westward from East Prussia.

Guderian had thus rapidly accomplished his first operational victory. Yet it would have been an easily obtainable objective for any competent commander and, once again, he inflated this accomplishment in his memoirs; although the German plan had called for the annihilation of the Polish forces in the Corridor, the bulk of the defenders had already side-stepped Guderian's forces and retired to the south.[11] Those unable to escape conducted a skilled fighting retreat northward, where they fell back on the formidable defensive strength of the Hel peninsula. Here, they would defy all German efforts to overrun them and hold out until the Polish capitulation.[12] The protracted and determined Polish defense of the Hel peninsula demonstrated that the XIX Motorized Corps had far from crushed the enemy opposition. Since the cutting of the Corridor was inevitable, the real question was how long could the Poles delay it? Certainly Guderian had forced the Corridor quickly, but he had done so only at the expense of not destroying the enemy that confronted him.

That September 5th was a momentous day for Guderian: he gave a tour of the battlefield to Hitler, Himmler, and Hitler's field headquarters commander, an infantry officer named Erwin Rommel. Guderian showed to Hitler what he now claimed to be the dominant weapon of modern war—armor. Hitler was undoubtedly impressed. The next day Guderian shifted his corps across East Prussia to participate in the advance on Warsaw. The original invasion plan had called for the XIX Corps to launch an attack due south on Warsaw, but the tough Polish resistance north and northwest of the capital led to a fortuitous change of plan. That night Guderian slept in a bed that Napoleon had once slept in at Finkelstein Castle, and he was so anxious to use any opportunity to exercise the ancient aristocratic privileges of the Prussian *Junker* that the very next evening, while his troops went into action, Guderian went off deer hunting. It would not be the last time that deer hunting would play a conspicuous role in his military career.

With the XIX Corps, reinforced by the 10th (the newest and as yet incomplete) Panzer Division, debate now swirled over the most appropriate axis of advance. The commander of Army Group North, Fedor von Bock, wisely wanted to swing to the southeast to avoid the enemy and harness the greater mobility of his armored and motorized forces, but the High Command rejected his request since it was privy to information that neither he nor Guderian had—the terms of the secret protocol to the Ribbentrop-Molotov Pact and the impending Soviet invasion of Poland from the east. Since the exact demarcation line between the future German and Soviet occupation zones was as yet undecided, the High Command was reluctant to allow its forces to advance too far east. Thus, when it issued new orders to resume the offensive on 8 September, it ordered Army Group North to adhere to the original plan and attack due south on Warsaw. Guderian vigorously protested this restriction but to no avail; he very vociferously and publicly rebuked his superior, von Bock, unaware that von Bock was passing on orders from above and against which he had already repeatedly protested to no avail.

Meanwhile the spearheads of Army Group South had smashed through the main Polish defenses in western Poland, inflicting heavy losses on the enemy. They were approaching the Vistula south of Warsaw and would soon reach the Polish capital. It appeared that

Guderian would be sorely disappointed that all the glory would go to Cavalry General Hoepner and the panzer commanders of Army Group South. But the 4th Panzer Division, the vanguard of the Army Group South received a drubbing when it tried to enter Warsaw unsupported. This combined with considerable resistance before the Vistula and northwest of the capital, astride the Bzura River, led the High Command to change its plans and adopt von Bock's original proposal to strike toward the southeast. Contributing to this change was an agreement with the Soviets outlining a provisional demarcation line that was farther east than originally envisioned. Circumstances once again provided Guderian with an unprecedented opportunity to conduct a long-range strategic deep penetration of the Polish rear.

Reinforcing Guderian's command with a second, albeit incomplete, armored division was not without cost, however. For, this division had previously supported the steady advance of the neighboring XXI Corps to the northeast. But once denuded of armored support, XXI Corps's advance stalled in the face of tough resistance. And even with the added support of the 10th Panzer Division, the XIX Corps began with an uneven start when it resumed the offensive on 9 September. The 18th Polish Infantry Division offered stiff resistance and the 20th Motorized Division quickly floundered. Guderian was induced to divert the 10th Panzer Division from its intended deep penetration to provide assistance. As he advanced southeast toward the Bug River, he exposed his left flank and rear to interdiction from Polish forces screening Grodno and Bialystok.[13] Although Guderian disingenuously dismissed this threat in *Panzer Leader* as insignificant, Polish forces did, in fact, launch a counterattack on 11 September and cut his line of communication, isolating Guderian (who was forward with the spearhead) from his corps headquarters.[14] But timidity characterized the Polish response and they failed to take full advantage of the opportunity that presented itself. Nonetheless, Guderian's reckless desire to be at the forefront of the action placed him in avoidable danger, and with all of Guderian's forces fully committed, von Bock was forced to divert elements of the XXI Corps to close the gap and extricate Guderian and his spearhead from its predicament. The danger was, therefore, greater than Guderian implied in his memoirs.[15]

On 13 September, Polish resistance finally weakened enough for Guderian's panzer divisions finally to gain operational mobility. By this juncture there were no mobilized Polish forces left, as all available reserves had been sent to defend the Polish capital and the Vistula Line. This allowed Guderian to effect an operational penetration of the Polish front. As Guderian drove deep into the Polish rear he now encountered troops of lower caliber. These were Polish reservists who were unable to offer significant resistance, in part because they were still mobilizing and in part because they lacked the heavy weapons capable of stopping a concentrated armored advance. Guderian's spearheads overran several Polish formations while they were still forming up.

By 14 September, the XIX Corps had reached Brest Litovsk, which showed no signs of surrendering as the garrison hunkered down in the city's strong ancient defenses. On 16 September, Guderian launched an mechanized attack on the city, attempting to take it by *coup-de-main*. Resistance was fierce and Guderian made limited progress. Polish resistance was broken only the next day by the approach of Soviet troops. More fearful of the communists than the Nazis, the garrison launched an abortive breakout attempt and when that failed, Guderian issued an ultimatum with a choice between surrender to the Germans or capture by the Soviets, the garrison promptly capitulated to the Germans. Guderian had made his first capture of a major city but without having to make an all-out fight for it. Here it must be emphasized the enormous impact of the sudden deep Soviet advance into the Polish rear, which destroyed all hopes of effective Polish resistance and correspondingly shattered Polish morale. Polish forces began to surrender *en masse* to Guderian's troops as they advanced south to avoid falling into Soviet hands.

On 15 September, von Bock ordered Guderian to split his XIX Corps and send one half of it northeast toward Slonim and the other southeast under the control of the newly inserted Fourth Army, commanded by Günther von Kluge.[16] Once again, Guderian immediately and vehemently protested this order at his first meeting with von Kluge—a politically insensitive way to begin the relationship. Because of Guderian's impetuosity, arrogance, and tactlessness, Guderian's relations with both von Bock and von Kluge quickly soured. Yet Guderian's distrust of von Kluge and von Bock was not reciprocated despite Guderian's perceptions to the contrary.[17] Both his superiors recognized his accomplishments and recommended him for the award of the Knight's Cross.[18] Unfortunately, Guderian came to hate von Kluge in Poland with a marked animus that never altered. It is hard to comprehend Guderian's enduring rancor toward von Kluge, beyond reading it as a fundamental clash of two strong-willed personalities. After all, von Kluge had only passed on the message from von Bock that so rankled Guderian. Moreover, he had acceded to Guderian's petulant demands and never issued the order Von Bock had given him. Throughout their tempestuous relationship, it was always von Kluge who acted as the conciliator as Guderian, the prima donna, always refused to forgive or forget the past.[19]

Throughout Guderian's description of the Polish campaign in his memoirs, we discover his usual disingenuousness. Just one example will suffice here. In his memoirs, Guderian implied that his spearheads met the spearheads of Army Group South in the dying days of the campaign, thus effecting the giant strategic encirclement that the original invasion plan had envisaged.[20] In actuality, his spearhead never established physical contact with Army Group South before the Polish surrender.[21] It was admittedly only a slight misstatement but—ever the propagandist—Guderian saw a slight distortion of the truth as a legitimate means of vindicating his vaunted armored forces.

To summarize the performance of the XIX Corps in the Polish campaign: Guderian's command advanced over 200 miles in ten days. His personnel losses were light, given his accomplishment: a 4 percent casualty rate. A much more telling statistic, however, that speaks volumes about Guderian's recklessness, is that fully 43 percent of Army Group North's entire campaign fatalities occurred within Guderian's corps: statistically, the XIX Corps suffered fatalities at three times the rate of Army Group North as a whole.[22] Serving under Guderian was therefore a particularly deadly honor.

Again, the deep penetration Guderian made from East Prussia into the Polish rear was certainly the most significant German strategic accomplishment of the campaign. But was it as important, or was his leadership as brilliant, as he implied in his memoirs? The push across the Polish Corridor into East Prussia outflanked the main

Polish defenses, leaving Guderian to face predominantly Polish reservists. Moreover, it was the Soviet invasion of Poland that decisively broke the backbone of Polish resistance, substantially aiding Guderian's advance. Thus, good fortune had smiled on Guderian: he had been in the right place at the right time.

With typical German thoroughness, the army minutely examined the Polish campaign and concluded that the performance of its mechanized forces had been below expectations. The panzer division's exclusively offensive training had ensured that they performed poorly on the few occasions when they had been forced on the defensive, and that they proved inept at night, forest, and urban warfare.[23] Most serious was the attrition rate that became evident after the campaign. The brevity (five weeks) of the campaign had initially distracted attention from the fact that, by its conclusion, much of the German armor had been rendered nonoperational and many tanks—including more than half of Guderian's—needed extensive workshop or factory repair.[24] After-action reports concluded that a longer campaign would lead to a dangerous diminution of armored capability.[25] But these warnings went unrecognized during the jubilant celebration that followed the dismemberment of Poland.

Though the XIX Corps withdrew from Poland before the murderous police and SS-TV (*Tötenkopfverbände*—"death's head") squads began their brutal ethnic cleansing campaign,[26] Guderian learned of these activities from his eldest son, Heinz-Günther, who reported on the concentration of Jews in ghettos and the "special handling" extermination operations and other horrors he personally witnessed during the fall of 1939.[27] It is unlikely that Guderian felt any more sympathy for the plight of Poland's Jews than he did for the Poles themselves. Certainly there is no record of his lodging any protests, as there are for the army commander of occupied Poland, Colonel-General Johannes Blaskowitz, whose repeated protests about SS and police atrocities and whose attempts to prosecute individuals responsible for war crimes earned him the enduring enmity of Hitler.[28] Guderian, however, had more important tasks at hand. He was frantically refitting the XIX Corps for the impending invasion of the west that Hitler was determined to launch before winter arrived.

Guderian continued to build up the armored force. He bitterly

protested efforts to divert resources from the armored force to supporting arms. Though he had personally witnessed the difficulties
caused by the lack of mobile-infantry fire support for his truck-borne
infantry in Poland, he opposed efforts to enhance its capabilities.
When the performance of the infantry in Poland was assessed as below par and the OKH demanded greater firepower and mobility to
allow the infantry to keep up with the mechanized formations,
Guderian resisted the most expedient solution, namely a self-propelled 150mm infantry gun. As the puny Panzer I tank came back
for factory overhaul during the fall of 1939, thirty-eight of them,
forming six independent companies, were so converted to self-propelled
guns. Yet Guderian opposed even this paltry diversion of armored
resources![29] When he lost this fight, he shifted gears and demanded
that these vehicles instead be assigned to the motorized infantry regi-
ments of his panzer divisions. Here he was successful: all six companies
fought with panzer divisions in the western campaign. In subsequent
campaigns they proved a valuable addition to the firepower available
to the (now renamed) panzergrenadiers of panzer divisions.

That fall Guderian also participated in a successful campaign to
scrap the light mechanized divisions and upgrade them to full panzer
divisions using newly produced tanks and the Czech tank plant captured that spring. But he lacked the institutional power to effect
such reorganization, because the post of Chief of Mobile Troops had
been dissolved as part of wartime mobilization. The future evolution
of the panzer troops now fell to the Commander of the Replacement
Army and the Chief of Army Production and Equipment, Colonel-
General Fritz Fromm, a situation that displeased Guderian. After-
action reports from Poland confirmed the low establishment and
inadequate staying power of the light mechanized divisions, and it
was owing to widespread army agreement—not Guderian's protestations—that the decision to upgrade the light mechanized divisions
to full panzer divisions was made.[30] The west was obviously a much
bigger theater than Poland and commanders widely recognized that
Germany needed more of the potent panzer divisions.

During October 1939, Guderian personally received the Knight's
Cross from the Führer. During the award ceremony, Guderian made
the mistake of saying that it was a good thing that Germany had

avoided a two-front war. Hitler was displeased, and perhaps this was the time that Guderian began to realize (and sympathize with) the intensity of Hitler's hatred of the Soviet Union. The Führer undoubtedly approved of Guderian's indomitable military spirit—he appeared to have been the kind of "National Socialist fighter" for whom Hitler yearned. Guderian believed, like Hitler, that the destiny of the German people would be determined by German feat of arms on the battlefield. Both men were correct, but the outcome would not be what they both expected and the human price for their hubris would prove staggering.

During the same month, the XIX Corps moved to Coblenz, where it went through frantic replenishing for an immediate invasion of the west during fall 1939. Hitler's insistence on pressing a reckless invasion of the west that fall sparked another major confrontation with his more conservative senior army commanders. Though Guderian was too lowly to play a direct role in these events, he was offended by Hitler's assault on the army's honor when senior commanders tried to dissuade Hitler from his reckless plan to immediately attack the west. Once again Guderian tried to continue his political detachment—a naive hope—given realities in Nazi Germany. He strenuously worked up his command to full operational readiness during the winter of 1939–1940 and incorporated the lessons learned from the Polish campaign.[31]

Guderian found himself brought into the strategic debate, which raged that winter. It was von Manstein—Guderian's contemporary at the 1907 War Academy—who suggested the thrust through the Ardennes that the Germans ultimately launched. Guderian was consulted on the feasibility of large tank forces passing through the Ardennes. Having spent time there in 1914 and 1918 Guderian confidently proclaimed that armored forces could penetrate the Ardennes. Only when he was subsequently informed that his motorized corps might spearhead such an invasion did Guderian immediately protest that his two panzer and single motorized divisions were inadequate for the task proposed. Ultimately, he would come to demand no less than seven mechanized divisions to penetrate the Ardennes.[32] With this force Guderian now claimed that he could not only break through the Ardennes but could fight his way across the Meuse and advance deep into France. This claim was widely met with derision, but, as whenever he was challenged, Guderian dug in his toes and obstinately defended his claims.

The new plan established a panzer group to spearhead the penetration of the Ardennes, comprising three motorized corps: the XLI, the XIV, and Guderian's XIX. The panzer group was assigned to Cavalry General Ewald von Kleist. Guderian received three panzer divisions plus the elite Grossdeutschland Motorized Infantry Regiment. The assembled force represented the greatest German concentration of armor yet seen in the war: 1112 of the 2438 panzer division tanks committed for the invasion of the west.[33]

Guderian tirelessly drove his troops forward as they conducted endless offensive training exercises during spring 1940. He analyzed, identified faults, and initiated corrective training, all with his characteristic energy.[34] Guderian was confident that the timidity of French strategic and tactical doctrine and the shallowness of the defenses in the Ardennes would ensure the success of the German forces.[35] He believed that adept tactical handling would allow his armored force to prevail over the slow and ponderous French. Once again he placed heavy emphasis on operational movement to outmaneuver rather than outfight the enemy; and he meticulously planned the rapid penetration through the narrow, winding Ardennes roads.[36] Again the key to the success of the penetration was the intimate cooperation between armor, panzergrenadiers, and engineers—the combined arms approach inculcated in German troops since the 1920s.

Once the campaign started Guderian was, as usual, in the thick of the action. He narrowly escaped a heavy French artillery barrage of his headquarters on 12 May and later that same day his light observer plane became lost and almost landed in French territory. A frequently practiced, combined-arms opposed amphibious assault crossing of the Meuse succeeded in the face of stiff, if ill-coordinated, French resistance on 13 May, though at substantial cost. Next, Guderian conducted his first major tank battle against two battalions of French light tanks that timidly counterattacked. The Germans outmaneuvered the more heavily armed and armored French tanks. During the next two days amid fierce fighting, they pushed aside the 3d French Armored Division at Stonne. Guderian began an immediate westward exploitation of his penetration of the Meuse, in contravention of von Kleist's orders. Breaking out into the French rear, Guderian's and Reinhardt's motorized corps wreaked havoc among French service echelons. As before, Guderian was in the thick of the action, commanding from the front and appearing at the main point of effort to push troops and commanders forward. With his habitual eagerness Guderian advanced his troops more quickly than the cumbersome French army could react. Indeed, his advance on 16 May, with just two panzer divisions generated alarm and consternation all the way up the German chain of command to Hitler. That evening, Guderian ignored a new stop order from von Kleist, precipitating a major argument between the two and von Rundstedt. Guderian immediately tendered his resignation, which von Rundstedt rejected, sending Colonel-General List, the Twelfth Army commander, to resolve the impasse: Guderian was given permission to conduct a "reconnaissance in force." Meantime, Charles de Gaulle's hastily improvised 4th Armored Division had hit Guderian's flank but was held off with some difficulty. Finally, on the 18th, Hitler regained his nerve and sanctioned the advance to the Channel coast.

But now even Guderian became cautious as he outstripped his logistics and faced a series of French counterthrusts, one of which penetrated to within a mile of Guderian's tactical headquarters before being repulsed. Once again, luck smiled on Heinz Guderian as the demoralized French resistance disintegrated before him. On 20 May the XIX Corps made the greatest one-day advance it would make in the campaign, thrusting forward fifty-six miles to reach the Channel coast near Abbeville, cutting the Allied armies in the west in two.

But where to go next? Having no more sense of the operational level of war than his peers, Guderian had not thought beyond the advance to the coast. With a long open southern flank inviting counterattack, opinion favored turning south to what was perceived by many to be the greater threat. It took a day for the German High Command to decide instead to turn north against the BEF (British Expeditionary Force). Late on 21 May, therefore, Guderian resumed the advance on Boulogne and Calais. It was at this juncture that the British launched their only major counterattack of the campaign; a small force counterattacked at Arras and inflicted appreciable losses on Rommel's strung-out 7th Panzer Division and the inexperienced SS Motorized Division Tötenkopf, elements of which fled in disarray.[37] But again the British effort represented too little, too late, even though it did instill nervousness in the Germans far greater than the meager resources committed.

Unfortunately, the one-day delay in renewing the offensive denied Guderian the opportunity to storm the Channel ports before the British established defenses for these vital points of evacuation; instead, he found the British prepared to offer a stiff fight for Boulogne. He pressed his advance toward Dunkirk, which would certainly have fallen in a day or two had not Hitler ordered Guderian's forces to stop. Fear of reverses—particularly the heavy tank losses that had accompanied the unsupported armored thrust into Warsaw the previous September—led Hitler to abandon the tank advance and order a halt to allow infantry to catch up and join XIX Corps for a renewed combined arms advance. Göring offered to finish off Dunkirk from the air, but this was only after the nervous Hitler had already decided to halt the advance. Once again, Guderian tried to subvert the stop order—co-opting his close SS commander friend, Sepp Dietrich, whom Guderian probably assumed was less likely to become a target of the Führer's wrath—to "improve their future jumping off positions," a common Guderian tactic quietly to continue offensive operations.

Hitler changed his mind on the 26th and ordered a general resumption of the advance, but the momentum of the German advance had waned and the Allies, rallying again as they found their backs to the sea, now offered determined resistance. Moreover, Guderian's forces had suffered 50 percent tank losses and were rapidly approaching the end of their endurance. Finally, on the 28th, Guderian appreciated that the moment had been lost. To prevent unnecessary casualties amid his precious armored forces, he also now advised abandonment of the armored advance and the reduction of Dunkirk by conventional infantry-artillery assault. The attendant delay allowed the bulk of the BEF and many French troops to be evacuated from Dunkirk. This was one of the things that Guderian forgot to mention in his memoirs.[38]

Hitler rewarded Guderian's dramatic accomplishment by conferring command of a panzer group on him for the next stage of the western campaign as the German military now turned to the attack across the Somme that sought to demolish the rest of the French military. Guderian's panzer group comprised his own XIX Corps and the attached XLI Corps. All together, he commanded four panzer and two motorized divisions. Yet Guderian's forces did not spearhead this offensive. It was Rommel's illustrious 7th Panzer Division that first broke through the French defenses on the Somme. The infantry assault that was to pave the way for Guderian began badly on 9 May and Guderian became embroiled in an argument with the Twelfth Army commander, General List, who thought Guderian was holding back panzer support because he wanted the infantry to fail. This incident illuminates the profound suspicion and distrust of Guderian that ran deep throughout the senior German officer corps and speaks volumes about the perception of Guderian as concerned only for himself. That List feared that Guderian would place the armored forces' own interests above all others just to be vindicated, even at the risk of defeat, tells us a great deal about the maverick, doctrinaire, panzer commander.

In retrospect, it can be seen that Guderian triumphed in France because, once again, he was at the right place at the right time. The Allied failure was strategic. Anticipating a repeat of the Schlieffen Plan, the Allies had committed themselves to forward deployment and engaging the enemy in Belgium and Holland, thereby drawing the bulk of the French strategic reserve from its central location (where, incidentally, it would have been perfectly positioned to halt Guderian's drive) northward into Belgium, denuding the vital Ardennes sector of reserves. Contrary to common belief, the Allies did not believe that the Ardennes was impenetrable to armored forces, only that no operational penetration could be achieved quickly without alerting the defenders and allowing them to bring up reserves to cordon off the penetration. In fact, the Allies invited a German penetration in such inhospitable terrain because they believed they could effectively pin down the German forces committed.

Moreover, undergunned and underarmored German tanks had had some nasty encounters with heavy French tanks near Rethel, as enemy armored forces began to regain some vitality and nerve. Then, once he had achieved a breakthrough, his armor penetrated deep into the French rear, heading southeast toward the Swiss frontier as French morale and resistance collapsed. In his private correspondence, Guderian expressed compassion for the plight of the French populace. This demonstrated that he held the "civilized" French in much higher regard than he did the Slavic Poles. Kenneth Macksey's claim that Guderian "was devoid of racial hatred" notwithstanding, it is evident that Guderian, like most Germans, felt more affinity for Western Europeans than Slavs.[39]

On 17 June, Guderian's fifty-second birthday, his spearheads reached Pontalier on the Swiss frontier. He had already swung to the northeast into Alsace to envelope the French army group defending the Maginot Line. The French sued for an armistice on 22 May. Germany had accomplished in six weeks what it had been unable to accomplish in the Great War and at a fraction of the cost. Guderian became a national war hero. He was allowed to broadcast a speech over the air to the entire German nation and he immediately set to work publicizing the accomplishments of the armored force, which he naturally viewed as the vindication of his dreams.

Flushed with success, Guderian looked for new, fresh conquests. He discussed "colonial questions" with General Ritter von Epp—an old *Freikorps* leader (and an inveterate Nazi). Clearly Guderian dreamed of unleashing his panzers to carve out a new German colonial empire in Africa. Guderian and von Epp, of course, also shared strong anticommunist beliefs. Von Epp had gained a reputation for slaughtering communists during the turbulent early days of the Weimar Republic. He was also chief of the Nazi Party's Department for Colonial Policy and was a member of Hitler's inner entourage.[40] Once again, Guderian's association with von Epp demonstrates Guderian's determination to curry favor with Hitler's intimates and gain access to his inner circle. Guderian was a man of great ambition who saw himself inherently destined for greatness.

Guderian was aware that Germany lacked the means to invade Britain directly and thus his attention turned to trying to force Britain to sue for peace by attacking and overrunning its colonial empire. Guderian assumed that he would be at the forefront of such a campaign. He also assumed that Hitler would rationally shift the *Schwerpunkt* of future operations to the Mediterranean in order to try to force Britain to the negotiating table. Guderian appreciated the necessity of taking Malta and landing in North Africa. He hoped to see Hitler commit up to six panzer divisions to overrun the British in Egypt. It is likely, given his personality, that Guderian was unhappy when Hitler chose Erwin Rommel to lead a small mechanized force (that would become the infamous Africa Corps) to North Africa with a defensive mission to buttress the wavering Italians.[41]

Again, Guderian showed his ignorance of the larger strategic picture, as he gave no thought to the immense logistical difficulties of supplying a mechanized army operating deep in North Africa. Guderian asked von Epp to intercede on his behalf and present his plan for invading Africa to Hitler, which he duly did. Hitler demurred—he was already preparing to confront the great ideological menace of Soviet communism. Guderian's political naiveté was such that he apparently had no premonition of where Hitler's attentions were turning, even though he had only to read Hitler's autobiography, *Mein Kampf*, to discern the ultimate direction that Hitler's aggression would take. Indeed, Guderian feigned surprise when he finally found out, or so he claimed years later, after the Soviets had defeated Germany.[42] Guderian claimed to have been perturbed by the specter of a two-front war. But his anti-communism left him happy to be off on campaign again against the Soviets. In reality, he offered minimal opposition to Operation Barbarossa and as he was instead selected to command a panzer group, he immediately immersed himself in the daily minutiae of readying his forces for the greatest challenge they would ever face—conquering Russia.[43]

Advance of Guderian's 2d Panzer Group into the Soviet Union, June–
December 1941.

Guderian and Operation Barbarossa, 1941

O N 22 June 1941, Guderian led the 2d Panzer Group, the strongest of the four German armored groups committed to Operation Barbarossa, into the Soviet Union. However, he was far from at ease with the daunting task that stood before him. He had reveled in the adulation that had followed his (apparently) stunning triumph in the west and in his reward of promotion to colonel-general, bestowed by Hitler on 19 July 1940. But conquest of the Soviet Union would require unprecedented strength and a major expansion of the armored force and substantial increase in the very modest tank production figures. Yet Hitler and the Nazi leadership, with a mixture of racist overconfidence, the intoxication of previous victories, and a pragmatic reluctance to unduly burden the German population, were unwilling to take the steps necessary to ensure success. Instead, Hitler's solution was to reduce significantly the number of tanks per panzer division and thereby double the number of panzer divisions in the year preceding Operation Barbarossa. The fact that Guderian was never consulted about halving existing divisional tank strength— he naturally strenuously opposed the measure—reveals the limits of his influence. His opposition reflected his continued preference for tank-heavy, rather than well-balanced combined-arms, mechanized formations.[1] Virtually every military historian since has sided with Guderian,[2] yet Hitler's organizational initiative actually created more and better-balanced armored formations, something that was an obvious necessity given the scale and scope of the envisioned campaign.

Moreover, the German armored force did acquire enhanced combat power through additional Panzer III and IV tanks that partially replaced the increasingly obsolete light Panzer I and II light tanks. A few additional armored half-tracks also came available, but they remained in very short supply. Limited production meant keeping the Panzer I and II in front-line service and substituting captured Czech Panzer 35(t) and 38(t) tanks for the missing mediums. Newly activated tank units formed from the large French arsenal captured in the West assumed occupation duties in Nazi-controlled Europe allowing Hitler to commit the bulk of Germany's meager panzer strength—some 3417 tanks—to Operation Barbarossa.[3]

It was not until November 1940 that Guderian became aware of Hitler's intention to invade the Soviet Union. He claimed in his memoirs to have been so dismayed by the risks of fighting a two-front war that he vehemently opposed Operation Barbarossa, but his objections were ignored.[4] Despite his supposed objections, Guderian fully participated in the contentious spring of 1941 strategic debates over Barbarossa.[5] Guderian firmly believed that the correct strategy would be to capture the political objective of the Soviet capital.[6] Nowhere did Guderian more clearly reveal his strategic myopia than in his stubborn belief that the capture of Moscow would collapse communist rule and end the war in the east. It was not until 1945 that Guderian began to recognize that only through psychological warfare and collaboration with anticommunist and anti-Russian forces within the USSR might Germany have stood even a remote chance of defeating a country of the size and resources of the USSR.

In May 1941 Guderian again willingly embraced and disseminated Hitler's official justification for aggression—that Barbarossa was a defensive preemptive strike and a noble undertaking to save Western civilization from being destroyed by the "Asiatic Bolshevik-Jewish menace." Guderian's actions thus intimate that by 1941 he had at least outwardly embraced the core tenets of national socialism—the necessity both of violent German expansion and of the destruction of the supposed Jewish-Bolshevik threat.[7] Moreover, throughout the war Guderian never seems to have given much thought to the profound consequences of the brutal ideological war of annihilation (*Vernichtungskrieg*) that Hitler ordered German forces to wage in the east.[8] For, German brutality drove the peoples of the USSR into the arms of their unpopular Stalinist regime and offered them no alternative but to fight to the bitter end, irrespective of the cost. Guderian, presumably blinded by anticommunism and racism, apparently never understood this most fundamental strategic reality of the war in the east.

But Hitler, not Guderian, dictated strategy; and Hitler gave Guderian the 2d Panzer Group, which comprised three motorized corps totaling five panzer, one cavalry, and three motorized divisions. It was deployed with the 3d Panzer Group to occupied Poland and assigned to Field Marshal Fedor von Bock's Army Group Center. Its mission was to thrust through the Soviet frontier defenses, destroy the Red Army and advance on Smolensk. Yet Guderian commanded fewer tanks than he had in May 1940 and his force was proportionately smaller than the one he had led in the previous summer. His was but one of four panzer groups given the mission of making deep strategic penetrations into the Soviet Union.

None of the panzer commanders—least of all Guderian—fully anticipated the impact of the immense Russian space. Armored forces would soon outpace their supporting infantry and be swallowed in the sheer size of the country. Moreover, designed for offensive operations, the panzer divisions were actually poorly organized and equipped for defense, as previous campaigns had amply demonstrated.[9] But in Russia they often found themselves unsupported and facing repeated Soviet counterattack both from trapped forces endeavoring to evade annihilation and from relief forces trying to rescue them.[10] Guderian's panzer group operated on a frontage in Russia that was often four times wider than he had experienced in France. In addition, from the beginning the Red Army fought fiercely, albeit often ineptly; and the bestial behavior of the Germans ensured that it did not lose its will to resist as the French forces had. More worrying still, the Soviets gradually learned from their grievous mistakes to fight more effectively.[11]

Even before the campaign began Guderian got embroiled in a tactical argument with von Kluge, the senior officer he had clashed with in Poland, who commanded the Fourth Army, to which the 2d Panzer Group was initially subordinated. Von Kluge wanted to have infantry achieve the initial break-in, to preserve his tank forces, which would then exploit the breakthrough. Guderian was determined to commit his armored group immediately to smash through the enemy, allowing maximum exploitation without loss of time. He immediately submitted their dispute to the Army Group Center commander, von Bock, who allowed the headstrong Guderian much freedom to execute operations as he saw fit and to commit his armor immediately as he desired.[12]

Guderian's squabble with von Kluge was both personal and professional. Von Kluge saw Guderian as a dangerous, impetuous innovator. Guderian saw von Kluge as intolerant, deceitful, and doctrinally opposed to maneuver warfare. He thus disliked von Kluge from the beginning and became ever more distrustful, his suspicion ultimately burgeoning into hatred. Von Kluge tried repeatedly to patch up their relationship, but was rebuffed each time by Guderian.[13] Their squabble was a fundamental clash between two different types of commanders—a calculating risk-taker versus a prudent, yet equally distinguished, commander.

Von Bock took the courageous stand of refusing to transmit the now infamous *Kommissarbefehl*, which authorized summary extrajudicial execution of Soviet political officers, to his subordinate commands.[14] In his memoirs Guderian claimed he never received or passed on the order. However, the evidence suggests otherwise. German war diaries indicate that the order was "almost universally followed"[15] and it is clear that some formations subordinated to Guderian's 2d Panzer Group definitely received the order, since they reported to Guderian's headquarters statistics on the numbers of commissars who had been summarily executed.[16] Guderian also claimed that he had refused to promulgate a directive that freed German troops from punishment for war crimes committed in the east.[17] In fact, just days into Barbarossa, his subordinate XLVIII Motorized Corps commander,

General Lemelsen, repeatedly issued orders clarifying who were legitimate targets for murder—namely, political officers and "partisans"—indicating that the troops under Guderian's command had correctly divined the Führer's desires and were enthusiastically engaged in often indiscriminate mass murder, even if they had not "officially" received such orders from Guderian in person.[18] Moreover, it is inconceivable that Guderian, as an officer who commanded from the front, was unaware of the wanton brutality. His silence on this subject —both at the time and later, in his memoirs—strongly suggests Guderian's acceptance of such brutality.

The available evidence suggests that one must reach the same conclusion about Guderian's knowledge of the mass murder committed by the *Einsatzgruppen* (Special Operation Groups) in his area of control during their *Sonderbehandlung* operations—literally "special handling," the Nazi euphemism for mass murder. The *Einsatzgruppen*'s standing orders required them to report to local army commanders, from whom they drew their supplies; so it is inconceivable that Guderian was not at least partially aware of their activities within his zone of command.[19] In fact, the SS and police commander responsible for *Einsatzgruppe* B that operated alongside Army Group Center reported "no difficulties" with any of the army commanders, which implies direct and willing cooperation from Guderian.[20] In fact, advance *Einsatzgruppen* detachments were attached on multiple occasions to front-line combat units of Army Group Center within Guderian's area of operations, for example, in the capture of Zhitomir.[21] In the light of this evidence, it is impossible to accept Guderian's postwar claim that he was ignorant both of their existence and the nature of their missions.

Despite the higher level of command and the far greater scale of operations in Russia—with his forces stretched over hundreds of miles—Guderian continued to lead from the front as he had always done, irrespective of the tactical and operational limitations of this approach. His solution to the problem of distance was simply to drive himself, his chauffeurs, and his staff twice as hard. Repeatedly, he came under direct enemy fire and on a number of occasions he had narrow escapes. But fortune continued to smile on him, at least for a while longer. Rapid deep penetration bypassed large enemy forces that then tried to exfiltrate their way back through Guderian's forces to safety. The inability of the German infantry to keep up allowed many of these encircled forces to escape. Guderian blithely pressed ahead, indifferent to what went on behind him, where the situation rapidly became much more fraught. Guderian believed in safety through movement, a precept that was of little comfort to the much less mobile infantry. But Hitler and many other senior commanders were hesitant (with good reason) and Hitler demanded that the pincers of the 2d and 3d Panzer Groups close around Minsk, rather than push on toward Smolensk as Guderian wanted.

In his personal diary Guderian was less enthusiastic about his early brilliant victories than he had been the previous year—a foreshadowing of what was to come. Guderian repeatedly wanted to press forward, while his superiors demanded intermittent pauses to let the infantry catch up and to round up and eliminate the still substantial enemy still fighting ferociously in the rear. Ultimately, millions were "mopped up," but hundreds of thousands more fought their way back to safety or simply melted away into local communities where they organized resistance groups, a process dramatically accelerated by the brutal extermination policies that the *Einsatzgruppen*, police, and rear-area security forces pursued in the occupied areas. Guderian clearly knew about such activities, but it is possible, if unlikely, that he did not understand their true scale and scope. At least, it seems he thought little of the negative consequences of such brutality, as he focused exclusively on the myriad details of daily operational command. Never did he articulate an understanding of the counterproductive nature of such actions. Indeed, as a virulent anticommunist Guderian had nothing but antipathy for Soviet communism and probably intellectually could not conceive how German policies could drive the Russian people into the hands of the Stalinist regime.

As the tactical situation developed without the emergence of any clear strategy, Guderian found himself subordinated to different armies Hitler began to issue poorly formulated orders to individual corps and operations focused on surrounding and annihilating those major enemy formations identified by intelligence (unfortunately, there were always more appearing, in part because of the poor quality of German intelligence).[22] Gradually over time and distance the panzer spearheads became increasingly dispersed, dissipating their inherent strength and leaving them vulnerable to counterattack.[23]

At the end of June, von Kluge ordered Guderian to stop temporarily. Guderian immediately conspired with Hermann Hoth, commanding the 3d Panzer Group, to press the advance on Smolensk, in defiance of von Kluge's halt order. Mother Russia came to the defenders' assistance as heavy rains and the sheer mass of Axis forces moving forward dissolved Russia's rudimentary road network into a morass of mud, dramatically slowing German forward movement. Gradually the Soviet defense gained more coherence and stiffened. As Guderian continued to ignore von Kluge's halt orders, the latter threatened Guderian with court martial. On 10 July, Guderian saw his first Soviet T-34 tank: he immediately recognized its superiority over existing German tanks, and this perturbed him, increasing his foreboding.

Moreover, Guderian's tank strength was falling off far more rapidly than in France. The greater distances, poorer roads, mud, dust, and sustained resistance all increased the attrition rate. Additionally, the repair and workshop echelons were equipped and prepared only for a short Blitzkrieg campaign, and spare parts were soon critically short. There were no local facilities for major overhaul, and most immobilized vehicles could not be shipped home at all, partly because of Soviet resistance and partly because of the slowness in converting the Soviet railway to German gauge. Thus, from early on, cannibalization was widely practiced to sustain operational strength.

As Army Group Center resumed its push toward Smolensk, relations between Guderian and von Kluge declined yet further. Guderian continued to subvert and evade direct orders from his commanding officer. On 9 July, he prepared to cross the Dnepr without orders, while his spearheads were already isolated and enemy strength was increasing. Guderian once again was given free rein by von Bock. In fact, attacks by bypassed Soviet forces were creating enormous difficulties for the follow-up infantry forces, but the impatient Guderian demonstrated complete indifference to the urgent military needs of von Kluge's other commands as he pressed ahead. His renewed advance effected another daring, deep, strategic penetration that closed around Smolensk a week later, thus isolating and annihilating another major enemy force. But the pace of the advance slowed as Soviet resistance increased. The German High Command also became complacent at the string of victories, failing to provide the reinforcement necessary to sustain the offensive power of the panzer groups and continuing to underestimate enemy resistance, resilience, and determination. The result was that the 2d Panzer Group experienced mounting deprivations as it advanced beyond the resupply ability of German logistics.

Guderian continued to command from the front despite the physical toll this style inevitably began to take on him. By mid-August even Guderian came to recognize the great strain he was under.[24] But, like most Germans, he naively continued to believe that the enemy was nearly broken and one last great offensive exertion would see Germany emerge triumphant. Amazingly, Guderian told Hitler on 4 August that the Red Army was scraping the proverbial bottom of its manpower barrel.[25] Yet, his frequent trips to the front must have revealed to him that such a perception was illusory.

Hitler ordered Army Group Center to pursue a diversion southward to Kiev in August, to assist in the capture of the Ukraine. But Guderian wanted to go straight to Moscow, because he continued to believe that capture of the Soviet capital would lead to the collapse of the regime. So entrenched was his opposition to this diversion of his command that he flew to meet Hitler at Rastenberg on 23 August. But he had no success, and in fact, he did not press his case, much to the fury of Franz Halder, the Chief of the General Staff. Macksey claims that Guderian realized he had no prospect of prevailing. Certainly he was not prepared to jeopardize his command position for principles. He thus gave in and submitted to Hitler's decision, much to Halder's intense irritation. Halder and Guderian had a serious breach over this incident, the latter believing that Guderian had unnecessarily capitulated. The damage to their relationship could never be repaired. Other historians, however, emphasize that Hitler essentially "bought off" Guderian, both by awarding him with the coveted Oak Leaves to his Knight's Cross on 17 July and by promising additional reinforcements.[26]

In fact, it was Guderian's superior, von Bock, who had a much more sophisticated strategic view: he recognized the necessity of organizing Russian forces to spearhead the overthrow of the regime under the guise of national liberation.[27] Never short of ambition, when a group of senior officers approached Guderian about becoming the new army commander-in-chief during August, he indicated his willingness to accept such a position.[28]

Guderian made every effort to make the Kiev diversion a success. Once again he ignored orders from his superiors as he pushed ahead at his own rapid pace. His attack gained surprise, as the Red Army had not expected an assault from the northwest, and Guderian drove his forces forward mercilessly, wanting to complete the operation as quickly as possible in order to resume an advance on Moscow. During his daring advance toward Kiev he encountered stiff resistance that threatened his exposed flank and caused a crisis. To extricate himself from this precarious situation, Guderian demanded reinforcements and resupply, further alienating von Bock, who had repeatedly warned Guderian of the flank threat.[29] Unknown to Guderian, von Bock, disillusioned with his mercurial subordinate, initiated discussions with Halder for Guderian's relief.[30] Yet on 16 September, the German pincers met at Lokhvitsa, concluding the largest encirclement of the war. This brilliant accomplishment stayed von Bock's hand temporarily. But time was now running out for Guderian.

Finally in mid-September Hitler issued orders to resume the drive on Moscow. But the 2d Panzer Group—like the rest of Army Group Center—was tired, depleted, and undersupplied, with little likelihood of resupply or reinforcement. Prudent voices, such as von Bock's, urged a temporary halt to offensive operations for the fall and winter. They argued that the *Ostheer* (Eastern Army) should go on the defensive and build up for a renewed effort against Moscow in the spring. Guderian was not one of these prudent voices; quite the contrary. What he failed to mention in his memoirs was that he the leading voice urging Hitler to make one last all-out bid to capture Moscow before the onset of winter. In fact, it was Guderian who convinced Hitler to resume the attack.[31] Never would Guderian's impetuous recklessness have more grave strategic consequences for Germany than in this high-risk gamble. Moreover, no action better demonstrated Guderian's strategic myopia than his adamant, erroneous belief that the entire Stalinist state would collapse if Moscow fell, because he simply could not understand how the brutality of the German invasion was inexorably stiffening Soviet resistance.

Guderian rapidly shifted his command from its southern deployment to face east and attack in record time. After an impressive feat of administration and organization, Guderian resumed his advance on 30 September, immediately broke through the surprised enemy, and advanced 130 miles to Orel in two days. But sterner tests now awaited: on 6 October, Guderian's 4th Panzer Division ran into substantial numbers of Soviet KV-1 and T-34 tanks at Mzensk. A titanic tank battle followed in which—probably for the first time in the war—the Germans experienced noticeable setbacks. Outclassed and outfought, Guderian was forced to halt his advance temporarily. Hitler's renaming of Guderian's command as the Second Panzer Army brought little help, because the strategic situation had swung against the Germans, and Guderian began to despair.[32] Winter snow followed, only to turn into mud that reduced the advance to a crawl. Troops endured ever-greater privations. Guderian had long shown great concern for the welfare of his men, and he became increasingly concerned about their dwindling morale and spirit.

Jubilant in success, Guderian did not take failure well, and he began to brood. He had always been characterized by pendulum swings between optimism and pessimism. So Guderian had eagerly grasped success and amplified it out of proportion, only to overreact and become depressed to see his elevated hopes inevitably dashed as the Second Panzer Army bogged down around Tula. It crept slowly onward until the very last moment—the evening of 4 December—as Guderian continued to send optimistic reports of his prospects of success.[33] Belatedly recognizing that the offensive was hopelessly stalled, however, on 6 December, Guderian unilaterally withdrew his spearheads into interim defensible positions, cognizant of an impending Soviet counterstrike.

Racially and ideologically dismissive of Soviet capabilities, Guderian and the other senior German generals underestimated the scale, scope, and savagery of the Soviet winter counteroffensive. In fact, Guderian bore substantial responsibility for the setback that was to come. His last desperate lunge for Moscow left the Second

Panzer Army unevenly deployed and therefore vulnerable to a counteroffensive against its greatly overextended southern flank.[34]
Guderian's attenuated and exhausted formations were forced to give
ground and demonstrated increasing signs of demoralization.[35] Without adequate transport and in terrible winter weather, quantities of
heavy weapons and supplies had to be abandoned, and the troops
suffered egregiously from frostbite.[36]

Guderian firmly believed in safety through movement—both in
offense and in defense—and he too willingly embraced withdrawal
by forces so weakened that they were incapable of such movement
without sacrificing their remaining combat power. Guderian now
pinned the responsibility on von Bock and von Kluge in an effort to
shift blame for these reverses. Again he used his family connections to
bypass von Bock's authority and communicate with the Führer in an
effort to get word of what he perceived to be the true state of affairs
to Hitler. Guderian entertained a fantasy that the officers around
Hitler were hiding the truth from him. Nothing could be further
from the truth: Hitler fully understood the realities at the front but
simply believed that willpower alone could surmount these obstacles
and wrest victory.

Just two days into the Soviet offensive, von Bock developed serious doubts about Guderian's ability to weather the crisis. Guderian
had proved too willing to retreat, even suffering severe casualties in
the process, while von Bock urged him to stand fast.[37] Contributing
to the deterioration of their relationship was Guderian's unwillingness to try to close the crucial gap west of Tula through which Soviet
forces drove deep into the army group rear.[38] Guderian thus began
withdrawing to the Susha-Oka River line in front of Orel and assumed command of the wavering neighboring Second Army, forming Army Grouping Guderian on 14 December.

On 17 December, Hitler ordered Guderian to stand fast and promised abundant reinforcements—a mix of a threat-and-reward tactic
that he would use with monotonous regularity until the end of the
war. On December 20, Guderian flew to Rastenburg to meet Hitler
and begged for permission to withdraw, explicitly criticizing Hitler's
strategy and leadership.[39] Hitler denied him permission: Guderian returned and proceeded with his withdrawal in flagrant disobedience

of Hitler's order. As the pressure mounted, the toll began to show: on 18 December, von Bock went on "sick" leave (but would return within the month to rescue Army Group South), and von Kluge, Guderian's implacable rival, replaced him.

New squabbles immediately broke out between Guderian and von Kluge. Again, the major issues were Guderian's repeated insubordination, his reluctance to assist in closing the disastrous Tula gap, and his refusal to accept personal responsibility for anything. Von Kluge quickly came to the same conclusion as his predecessor, that Guderian had lost his nerve, a conclusion that was not without merit. When Guderian defied von Kluge and abandoned Chern without orders and then tried to cover up his action, the two had a mighty altercation. An angry Guderian impulsively asked to be relieved, and von Kluge was more than happy to forward his request to Hitler on Christmas Day 1941, and Guderian was officially relieved the next day. Hitler did not stand up for Guderian—he was just another of those spoilt General Staff officers without the backbone and character to be expected of a true national socialist officer. More than forty generals shared a similar fate that winter.

Despite Kenneth Macksey's claim that Guderian "at this moment of ugliest adversity, had performed at his best," the reality was quite different.[40] In truth, Guderian proved too prone to retrograde movement with forces incapable of such action. This reflected his persistent belief in the superiority of maneuver. Moreover, Guderian was simply not a very effective defensive commander. He had not trained for or studied defense and considered it to be by far the inferior posture. Intellectually, therefore, he was opposed to Hitler's hedgehog defense and favored retrograde maneuver. But given the immobility of the German army—owing to lack of transport and minimal winter equipment—the only viable action was to stand fast in fortified village hedgehog defenses and weather the Soviet storm as Hitler demanded.[41] Any time German forces had fought delaying withdrawals they had found it difficult to disengage from the enemy—who was better equipped for winter warfare—without suffering appreciable losses, particularly heavy weapons that had to be abandoned for lack of transport and fuel.[42] Hitler was usually poor at strategic decision making, but he was right this time, although this would have disastrous consequences for the future, unfortunately, as it reinforced Hitler's sense of his strategic genius and infallibility. The problem with the retreat Guderian desired was that it would have turned into a rout since his attenuated, ill-supplied forces, ill-equipped for winter maneuver, were simply incapable of the operational maneuver he continued to advocate.[43] The "stand fast" orders Hitler gave thus helped save the Second Panzer Army from destruction.

That this was indeed the case is revealed by how the Second Panzer Army fared in the subsequent winter battles. Colonel-General Rudolf Schmidt took over Guderian's command and stood fast as ordered. He was the obvious choice because his aggressive style of defense had already extricated several encircled divisions, and he clearly had the stomach for this vicious, all-out fight.[44] Renouncing the retrograde maneuver that Guderian favored, Schmidt ordered his forces into positional defensive strongpoint hedgehogs, normally built around villages, in compliance with Hitler's orders. Schmidt then preceded to do what Guderian claimed was "impossible": he restored a new defensive front. Soviet forces destroyed their offensive strength butting against these stubborn defensive hedgehogs that maximized what residual fighting strength German forces retained. Standing fast saved significant quantities of heavy weapons that now, aided by the weather, clumsy Soviet attack doctrine, and offensive inexperience, took an increasing toll on the Soviet attackers. Immediate counterattack usually ejected Soviet forces that had infiltrated between the German defensive hedgehogs. At Sukhininci, for example, an encircled regiment of the 216th Infantry Division held off two Soviet divisions for more than a month until relieved by a local counterattack organized by Schmidt.[45] Once the Soviet offensive began to ebb in late January because of the sheer exhaustion of its forces, Hitler allowed Schmidt to make localized withdrawals to better defensive positions. By March Schmidt had successfully weathered the storm and restored a firm defensive front: the "impossible" had been accomplished.[46]

Although it was during that fall that Guderian developed his first doubts about Hitler's command ability, he primarily blamed von Kluge for his dismissal.[47] He likewise continued to hold the Army High Command responsible for the lack of supplies and winter clothing. In his memoirs he claimed that Hitler had been unaware of the extent of the logistical deficiencies prior to 20 December and Guderian unfairly took personal credit for the winter clothing collection drive organized by the Nazi Party that winter.[48] Yet, Guderian had failed to demonstrate the "eastern hardness" that Hitler thought essential in a good National Socialist officer. More than anything else it was his repeated, insolent defiance of higher authority, his insatiable and threatening demands for more of everything, his inability to understand the needs of other commands or act as a team player, combined with his inability to finesse his superiors, that cost Guderian his appointment. In retrospect, his repeated and flagrant disobedience of higher authorities alone was sufficient grounds for dismissal. That he thought it impossible to cobble together a new defensive front during late December demonstrated that Guderian had also fallen victim to the crisis of confidence that spread like wildfire through the *Ostheer* that winter. Consequently, he was no longer fit to command the Second Panzer Army. Throughout his career he displayed despondency when confronted with failure: this time such fatalism quite appropriately got him cashiered.

Inspector General of Armored Troops, 1943–1944

IN HIS memoirs Guderian glossed over his activities of 1942, when he remained on the unassigned officer reserve list. He had good reasons to omit details of his actions, since they did not reflect well on the self-image he wished to depict. Part of the time he spent receiving treatment and recuperating from heart troubles that the strain of the Eastern Front had exacerbated. When not receiving treatment, however, he was not idly kicking his heels—quite the opposite. Initially, Guderian spent some time looking for a house in southern Germany where he could live after retiring. Then his horizons widened, and he extended his search and began looking for a much more extravagant new home. This change occurred during the spring of 1942 after Guderian accepted a massive payment of 1.25 million marks from Hitler. To put the scale of this bribe in perspective, it was the equivalent of more than fifty years' regular salary for an officer of Guderian's rank and seniority![1] During the summer of 1942 Guderian traveled extensively around the Wartheland of West Prussia (annexed after the German conquest of Poland) with the staff of the local Nazi *Gauleiter*, or district leader, looking for a suitable Polish aristocratic home to appropriate. He found a spacious estate to

Lieutenant General Guderian (standing, left) participates in a celebration in the field with Hitler, senior German generals and officers of Lieutenant General Paul Otto's 13th Motorized Infantry Division near Eger, the Sudetenland on 3 October 1938. The meal is a celebration of the first day of the peaceful German "annexation" of the Sudetenland, following the signing of the Munich Treaty. The meal was pork stew with potatoes. Sitting two seats to the right of Hitler is General of Artillery Wilhelm Keitel, Chief of the Armed Forces High Command. *National Archives and Records Administration.*

Heinz Guderian and officers from his corps staff and panzer troop commanders observe the forward advance of elements of his corps through Bouillon, Belgium, toward the Meuse River on Sunday, 12 May 1940. *National Archives and Records Administration.*

Heinz Guderian in Bouillon, Belgium, on Whitsunday, 12 May 1940, directing the forward advance of his XIX Motorized Corps toward Sedan and the Meuse River, the first primary objective for his command in the opening stages of the Western campaign. *National Archives and Records Administration.*

General of Armored Troops Heinz Guderian greets tanks from his XIX Motorized Corps on the roadside near le Quitteur, France, on 16 June 1940. In the foreground is a Nazi flag intended to mark the forward position of German troops for Luftwaffe ground attack planes. *National Archives and Records Administration.*

General Guderian confers with a staff officer near le Quitteur, France, on 16 June 1940. That day elements of the 1st Panzer Division had captured intact a bridge over the Saône River, but, unaware of this success, Luftwaffe planes repeatedly—but unsuccessfully—attacked the bridge. *National Archives and Records Administration.*

Colonel General Guderian participates in one of a series of pre–Operation Barbarossa planning exercises held at the Army High Command headquarters at Zossen outside of Berlin during early June 1941. Here he is probably observing proposed deployments on a large map table. *National Archives and Records Administration.*

Heinz Guderian consults with other officers at a pre–Operation Barbarossa planning session at Zossen sometime in early June 1941. During these war games, serious operational disputes between the panzer commanders and other generals were ironed out, though at some cost. Guderian had to accept temporary subordination of his Second Panzer Group to the Fourth Army, commanded by his nemesis, Field Marshal von Kluge. *National Archives and Records Administration.*

Colonel General Heinz Guderian, commander of the Second Panzer Group, visits the headquarters of the 29th Motorized Infantry Division near Tolotschin, Russia, on 11 July 1941 to coordinate the XLVII Panzer Corps' exploitation of its successful forcing of the Dnepr River at Kopys, south of Orscha, the previous day. *National Archives and Records Administration.*

An official, and probably posed, photograph taken on 22 February 1943 to commemorate Guderian's return to active duty and his promotion by the Führer to the position of Inspector General of Armored Troops, the final details of which were then being sorted out. The picture was taken at the "Wolf's Lair," Hitler's field headquarters near Rastenburg in East Prussia. *National Archives and Records Administration.*

A portrait of Colonel General Guderian wearing the black uniform of the panzer troops. At his throat is the Knight's Cross with Oakleaves. The picture was taken probably during 1943–4. *National Archives and Records Administration.*

General of Armored Troops and Knight's Cross recipient Heinz Guderian, accompanied by Organisation Todt (paramilitary construction corps) leaders, marches past German civilians during a victory parade in an unidentified German town, date unknown. *National Archives and Records Administration.*

General Inspector of Armored Troops Colonel General Guderian receives congratulations from Adolf Hitler as other senior officers salute. The officer next to Guderian, his face obscured, is Dr. Karl-Otto Saur, the Director of the Technical Office of the Armaments Ministry. The picture was taken between 1943 and 1944. *National Archives and Records Administration.*

Colonel General Heinz Guderian converses with Reich Minister of Economics Dr. Walter Funk. The topic of conversation may well be Guderian's insistent demands for increased production of armored vehicles. The location is possibly the "Wolf's Lair" in Rastenburg, East Prussia. Date unknown. *National Archives and Records Administration.*

Heinz Guderian looks on while Grand Admiral Raeder, head of the Kriegsmarine, greets Reichsmarschal Hermann Göring, head of the Luftwaffe. Probably taken on 22 May 1940, the day that Boulogne was captured. *National Archives and Records Administration.*

Heinz Guderian converses with Reichsmarschal Hermann Göring, while Admiral Raeder looks on, to Guderian's right. The body language suggests a frosty discussion. Guderian disliked Göring and had a negative attitude toward the Luftwaffe in general. Probably taken on 22 May 1940, the day that Boulogne was captured. *National Archives and Records Administration.*

Colonel General Heinz Guderian, in the black uniform of the armored troops, converses with SS *Obergrüppenfuhrer* (General of the Waffen-SS) Hans Jüttner, the head of the SS Operational Main Office. As Inspector General of Armored Troops, Guderian long sought full control over the panzer units of the Waffen-SS but was never able to gain it. Date unknown. *National Archives and Records Administration.*

his liking, but Hitler's Chancellery Office (which dispensed these secret funds) rejected his application to take possession because it was too excessive and would establish a bad precedent.[2] He therefore had to look for a more modest estate and in October 1942 finally settled on possession of a large twenty-five-hundred-acre rural estate of excellent farmland at Deipenhof. The final obstacle to Guderian's moving in was the forcible eviction of the Polish owners.[3] In fact this "bribe" (which is precisely how Hitler conceived of it, distrusting the senior generals and thinking it necessary to bribe them to keep them in line) represented the largest single bribe that he ever gave to any of his field commanders.[4]

In fact, Guderian had already been receiving special, regular, tax-free monthly payments of 2000 Reichsmarks—effectively doubling his gross salary[5]—since August 1940, after he was promoted to colonel-general in the aftermath of the successful western campaign. Such "honorific reimbursements" were specifically designed to bind senior military officers to Hitler and the Nazi state. Guderian's payments alone represented three times the annual salary of an army major, and no less than eight times the salary of a sergeant.[6] Moreover, given that these bonuses were tax-exempt and that wartime Germany's income tax rates reached as high as 65 percent, these secret bonuses massively increased Guderian's net salary. These illegal bribes were paid out a secret Chancellery "discretionary account" and were intended, according to Hitler, to overcome officers' "inner convictions" so that they became compliant servants of the Nazi regime.[7] They worked.[8]

Guderian was well aware of the unorthodox and precarious nature of these payments: that they came directly from Hitler, through secret Chancellery channels, and could be withdrawn at any moment by Hitler himself.[9] These payments continued throughout Guderian's 1942 consignment to the officer reserve at Zossen, indicating that Hitler generally continued to view Guderian favorably on the whole and leading him to anticipate future re-employment. Certainly, the continuation of such payments throughout 1942 tempered whatever bitterness Guderian felt at his dismissal. Guderian was explicitly discouraged from engaging in written correspondence regarding any matter concerning these bribes and had to sign a confidentially agreement before receiving the funds. He was completely aware that Hitler was bribing him.[10] The strongest evidence that he knew he took bribes was his failure to mention such payments in his memoirs.

In his memoirs Guderian defended his grandiose move up to the Junker aristocracy (at least in appearance) on the grounds that he was homeless, having lost his dwelling in Berlin to Allied bombing. Guderian apparently gave no thought to the fate of the previous Polish landowners who had been dispossessed—victims of the brutal Nazi "resettlement" and "Aryanization" programs implemented in occupied Poland. Again, this is consistent with his antipathy toward the alien "Slavic" Poles. Thereafter Guderian played the role of a provincial Prussian aristocrat. His ego and ambition are apparent in references to this matter in his personal correspondence, in which he constantly complained of what he considered to be the insufficiency of his gift from the Führer, even though it was the largest Hitler ever made to a military commander.[11]

His acquisition of Deipenhof in West Prussia also reflects Guderian's strategic myopia, given that it was located on the eastern periphery of Germany and vulnerable to the advance of the Russian military. Guderian continued to believe in his Führer and in ultimate German victory.[12] At Deipenhof Guderian adopted the traditional pursuits of the Junker: he purchased livestock and began breeding. By all accounts, he loved embracing the lifestyle of his ancestors.

But Guderian's ego and ambition prevented him from forsaking his military career in favor of the life of a gentleman farmer. Throughout 1942 he worked diligently toward reinstatement. When he came to appreciate that he had fallen, at least temporarily, out of the Führer's favor, he had personal and professional contacts intercede on his behalf. In particular, he worked his family connections: during September 1942 he pressured his relative by marriage Bodewin Keitel, head of the army personnel department, to try to get him reappointed. When Keitel was himself replaced, Guderian studiously cultivated a warm relationship with his successor, Colonel-General Rudolf Schmundt. Guderian also worked old friendships with key Nazis. The most important of these was Sepp Dietrich, who moved in Hitler's inner circle. Guderian succeeded in persuading Dietrich to intercede with the Führer on his behalf. Dietrich in his typical blunt fashion told Hitler that Guderian had been unfairly treated during his dismissal.[13] Their friendship continued and deepened, contributing to the growing perception among military and political circles that Guderian was, and long had been, a Nazi sympathizer.

In seeking a reappointment, Guderian faced less opposition from Hitler than from senior German commanders with whom he had had confrontations in the past. But a few powerful friends continued to lobby on his behalf. Primary among them was the new chief of the army personnel department, Schmundt, who worked hard behind the scenes to overcome suspicion and hostility toward Guderian and lobby for his return to command. It is interesting that Schmundt emphasized Guderian's fealty to the Führer and Party during these efforts.[14] Yet Hitler's deep-seated mistrust of his generals—particularly ones he had sacked—delayed Guderian's reappointment.

Also that year, other people were seeking Guderian. These were members of the anti-Hitler resistance, hoping that his dismissal had turned him against Hitler as it had other commanders, such as Beck. Infantry General Friedrich Olbricht cultivated a friendship with Guderian and tried to persuade him to join the conspirators. In fact, at least four conspirators contacted Guderian during 1942. But Guderian remained steadfastly ambivalent. He strongly opposed the idea of the assassination of Hitler, the legitimate sovereign leader of Germany, who Guderian still considered to be a great leader to whom Germany's national destiny was inexorably tied and with whom Guderian had no inclination to break. Moreover, he held profound doubts about the individuals involved in the conspiracy under Beck's leadership. Guderian simply did not consider Beck the kind of man of decisive action necessary to accomplish a dangerous coup. And he remained true to his Prussian oath of loyalty that he had sworn directly to Hitler himself. (It also is possible that Guderian believed that he, not Hitler or any replacement preferred by the conspirators, was the great leader that could save Germany.) Thus for both moral and pragmatic reasons, Guderian kept the conspirators at a distance, while simultaneously committing treason by failing to report their conspiracy to Hitler. It has been alleged that, although ambivalent, Guderian nonetheless contacted a few other generals—a dangerous undertaking—without finding support. Whether Guderian really did discuss conspiracy with anyone is impossible to ascertain, but it is known that he was contacted and that he promised to keep quiet. The conspirators, however, worried by Guderian's image as a Nazi loyalist, threatened him both with physical harm and with disclosure of his participation in these treasonous conversations.

Guderian was still confident that he would be recalled and that through dint of his brilliance, the mistakes of Hitler and the Nazi leadership could be corrected so that Germany could win the war. Fortunately for Guderian's military career, in 1942 the tide of battle inexorably turned against Germany. The *Ostheer* had barely weathered the winter before Hitler ordered a grand new summer offensive: Operation Blue. Despite great initial success, it stalled before Stalingrad and in the Caucasus and ended with the disastrous encirclement and annihilation of the Sixth Army at Stalingrad during the winter of 1942–3. Moreover, 1942 had proved a bad year for the German armor force. Tank production had increased steadily, but not fast enough, as a third generation of formidable German tanks— the Panther and the Tiger I—emerged after difficult development. But their enemies still produced many more tanks than the Germans. Guderian had warned of the growing numerical disparity just before his departure and in 1942 had urged increased tank production and the rapid development and production of improvised tank destroyers (*Panzerjäger*) that married existing tank guns in open mounts to obsolete tank chassis to create self-propelled antitank guns. That year also saw the up-gunning and up-armoring of the existing Panzers III and IV to maintain their combat effectiveness. In addition, although designed for infantry fire support, the gunner's *Sturmgeschütz* assault guns were also up-gunned to provide mobile antitank defense for the infantry they supported. The new tanks, the upgraded assault guns, and the improvised *Panzerjäger* together temporarily ameliorated the increasing disparity between German and Allied tank power.

After the disastrous strategic defeats of the winter of 1942–3, average operational tank strength in Russia fell to a mere twenty-seven vehicles per armored division. Hitler, temporarily shaken by these setbacks (he had, after all, assumed personal command of forces on the southern sector during the winter of 1942–3), finally, albeit temporarily, recognized that the armored force needed a strong-willed dynamic subordinate to revitalize it, even if that meant someone that had a reputation for being difficult. Out of desperation, during February 1943, Hitler had uncharacteristically given Erich von Manstein, the commander of Army Group South, an unprecedented degree of operational freedom in his efforts to check the Soviet advance into the Ukraine. This had brought temporary operational success and led to the recapture of Kharkov. Schmundt and others renewed their urgings to recall Guderian with unprecedented powers to galvanize armored production and revitalize the striking power of the armored force and now finally persuaded Hitler to recall him.

In response to initial queries about whether he would be willing to return with the title of Inspector General of Armored Troops, rather than being thankful at the prospect of being re-employed at all, Guderian held out for enormous power and authority. Guderian had a personal interview with an undecided Führer on 20 February, while von Manstein's counterstrike was progressing nicely. Hitler remained uncertain and ambivalent, however, but ultimately decided that he needed Guderian. Guderian demanded the full range of powers that had been denied him in November 1938, when he was appointed Chief of Mobile Troops. He claimed that he would need such power in order to make the armored branch into a decisive war-winning instrument. The result was a new armored force that answered directly to Hitler, another army within an army. Hitler gave Guderian, as Inspector General of Armored Troops, wide-ranging authority over the formation, activation, and training of armored units of all the armed services, including the Luftwaffe and Waffen-SS. He also quickly established a close collaborative relationship with Albert Speer regarding the future technical development of armored fighting vehicles. Moreover, he received responsibility for the development of armored warfare doctrine and tactics, as well as command of mechanized replacement and training units, schools, and establishments, all formerly the responsibility of the Replacement Army.

Thus, on 1 March 1943, Guderian succeeded in his lifelong ambition of dominating armored warfare evolution in Germany, as the panzer troops became an autonomous branch within the German armed forces. Such was Guderian's ego and self-confidence that he never doubted for a second that he was fitted for such a task. Because he was determined, he would succeed in creating his vision at any price.

No one had previously succeeded in acquiring such military authority from Hitler as Guderian. But he did not get everything he wanted, any more than anyone in Hitler's Germany did. He did not wrest control of assault guns from the artillery, for example. In the months following Guderian chafed over these minor limitations rather than embracing and recognizing his enormous accomplishment. Not content with the power Hitler had conferred upon him, Guderian precipitated a revival of the damaging turf wars that had hindered evolution of mechanized forces in the late 1930s as he renewed in 1943 the bitter battle to obtain complete control over all assault guns, which would have denied the artillery of its most mobile and effective infantry support weapon. The fundamental problem was that, when upgraded in 1942 with the long-barreled 75mm gun of the Panzer IV tank, the StuG III assault gun became a potent tank destroyer. Having no turret and a low silhouette, assault guns proved perfect for the defensive armored operations in which the army now found itself engaged. They were lighter and took about 30 percent fewer resources to construct than a Panzer IV tank; assault guns thus provided a workable solution to Germany's ever-growing tank shortage, but in turn, the diversion of assault guns to armored units both challenged the artillery's traditional central role in the Wehrmacht and eroded the gunners' ability to provide the kind of infantry fire support that grenadiers needed. Gunners rightly resisted Guderian's efforts to usurp absolute control of assault guns. Since he had failed to gain control of them when he accepted his new appointment, he now opposed their increased production and instead demanded control over the future development and procurement of assault guns. This was a foolish move when Germany was so short of armor, since ten StuG III assault guns could be constructed for the time, resources, and cost of seven Panzer IV tanks, though they carried the exact same armament and had comparable performance for the defensive warfare in which Germany now found itself increasingly engaged. In his opposition to increased assault gun production, Guderian overstated the advantages that the full rotating turret of battle tanks held over assault guns in terms of flexibility and general purpose.[15]

The gunners proved much more flexible than Guderian. Since early 1943 they had voluntarily relinquished assault guns to constitute new assault gun batteries in infantry divisional antitank battalions to augment their defensive firepower.[16] They even relinquished assault guns to re-equip panzer units during the Stalingrad crisis of the winter of 1942–3.[17] Guderian managed to wrestle from the gunners an allocation of 100 assault guns per month in May 1943 to re-equip depleted panzer and *Panzergrenadier* divisions.[18] Though he never succeeded in gaining complete control of assault guns (nor should he have), military necessity, rather than Guderian's leadership, was largely responsible for their increasing utilization in defensive anti-armor roles.

With his great organizational abilities Guderian immediately breathed fresh life into the languishing armored force with his classic vigor and clear-sightedness. One of his first moves was to improve basic data collection: astonishing as it seems, initially Guderian was unable to ascertain the actual inventory of German armor owing to lax record keeping. Very quickly he established improved procedures to allow regular, systematic tracking of production, distribution, combat losses, and inventory of all armored fighting vehicles.[19] He then presented a new production plan on 9 March, only one week after taking office. It offered to rationalize armored production with maintained production of existing vehicles, while new third-generation tank designs were finalized, and abandoned flights of fancy Hitler loved, such as the unrealistic Mouse super-heavy tank. But sectional interests won out in the struggle for armor assets. The gunners kept most of their assault guns, and Hitler overruled Guderian's attempt to thwart future creation of air force and SS mechanized forces, a decision that clearly fell within the remit of the Führer.

Guderian staffed his Berlin headquarters on Bendlerstrasse with combat-experienced armor officers. For his chief of staff he chose the talented Wolfgang Thomale, an exceedingly capable organizer and staff officer. Thomale played an ever greater role in developing the panzer force because Guderian could not abandon his "hands-on" approach to problem solving, which constantly took him away from headquarters to the tank factories, training commands, higher headquarters, and formations in activation or reconstitution. Much of the day-to-day running of his headquarters Guderian effectively left to Thomale, something he again failed to acknowledge in his memoirs.

As Inspector General, Guderian repeatedly worked himself to the point of exhaustion. He frequently erupted with anger and invective toward others, as his ego grew proportionate to his elevation in rank. Almost immediately Guderian clashed with Colonel-General Fritz Fromm, the Commander of the Replacement Army, as he demanded new revised establishments be created for panzer divisions and opposed diversion of resources to SS and Luftwaffe mechanized units.[20] It is interesting that in his memoirs, while railing at the gunners, Guderian was surprisingly mute in his criticism of SS and Luftwaffe opposition. It shows that he cultivated powerful allies amid the senior Nazi and state military leadership. Indeed, according to Walter Warlimont, the OKW Deputy Chief of Operations, Guderian "sought a closer association with the Party than was customary among other officers."[21]

In the comfort of Berlin, Guderian became highly critical of field commanders and ultimately imitated the constant barrage of complaint emanating from the Führer. He began to comprehend the damaging effect Hitler's war leadership was having on Germany's strategic position and the lack of logic and consistency in the methods being pursued to combat it. Guderian, the inveterate optimist, while worried by the deteriorating strategic situation, still believed in 1943 that Germany could win the war, if only he himself ran things and effectively contained the damage Hitler was causing.

But Guderian proved as strategically incompetent as his Führer: indeed, he understood little regarding grand strategy. He constantly sought more resources for his panzer troops at the expense of competing and just as valuable needs of the Luftwaffe, navy, and other army branches. He had no time for naval operations and displayed little interest in how the air war would impact ground operations. He was incapable of articulating a coherent, integrated interservice strategy that might rescue Germany from its dire strategic situation.

Instead, Guderian tried to limit Hitler's damaging impact on strategy and military operations, working through the chain of command in an effort to contain him and substitute his own leadership for that of the Führer's. It was a naive effort at best, one that only a man of Guderian's political naiveté and astonishing optimism and egoism could believe had any prospect of success.

A vexing question is what Guderian knew about the vicious exploitation of slave labor partly responsible for the dramatic increase
in war production during 1943–4, during his appointment as Inspector General of Armored Troops. He made repeated tours of the
tank production factories, as well as of occupied Europe; it is unthinkable that Guderian could have remained innocent of the hor-
rific crimes and the brutal reality of Nazi occupation. He visited steel
manufacturing factories and tank plants, all of which made extensive
use of slave labor drawn from the concentration camp system. Today
we know the harsh, brutal inhuman conditions under which slave
laborers worked in Germany and the high mortality rate that they
suffered.[22] Undoubtedly Guderian saw such workers and understood
what was occurring, but he raised no moral objection. He seems not
to have cared: to Guderian, the Machiavellian, the ends justified the
means. Their fate was apparently a necessary price for the improve-
ment of tank production that would allow the armored force to regain its vital strategic role to save Germany from defeat and win the
war, making Guderian one of the great generals of history. It is questionable if he recognized the fatal strategic repercussions on his country
of Nazi repression.

Yet Guderian ran into constant refitting problems. Hitler's desire
to raise new formations at home undermined Guderian's efforts to
reconstitute formations at the front. Guderian supported Hitler's
demand for maximum tank production and then criticized Hitler
because the focus on production meant minimal provision of spare
parts to keep tanks operational. The operational serviceability rates
plummeted and literally thousands of damaged tanks had to be sent
back to Germany for complete rebuilding (a process that could take
a year) after having been stripped of all useful parts by desperate
workshops trying to keep other vehicles operational.[23]

Because Hitler repeatedly directed mechanized forces into strategically senseless situations Guderian's efforts to rebuild the panzer
arm were hampered. Guderian opposed Hitler's planned summer of
1943 offensive, Operation Citadel at Kursk, because he had labori-
ously rebuilt the armored force during the spring of 1943 and believed that even success would bring substantial losses, which would
set back his efforts to rebuild the armored force. A defeat might weaken
his efforts to enhance and entrench his new power. He also recognized

the inevitable field adjustment problems that the new Panther and Tiger tanks and heavy Elefant and Nashorn tank destroyers would encounter in their first major operational deployments. Obsessed with the strategic potential of these new weapons, Hitler unwisely delayed the offensive for too long and retained excessive faith in what it could accomplish.

Instead, Guderian advocated maintaining a strategic defensive through 1943 but only so he could build up the armored force and consolidate his control over it. He showed little awareness of the deteriorating strategic situation—at sea, in the air, and on land—that indicated that this strategy could not reverse German defeat. Hitler simply shrugged off Guderian's passionate objections as sincerely felt but misguided.

An area where Guderian did often succeed was in his accumulating influence among the decision-making elite of Nazi Germany. There can be little doubt that he was a consummate political operator. Whatever manipulation enhanced his position he tried, including removal of Wilhelm Keitel, his cousin-in-law. He cultivated Goebbels acquaintance so successfully that the latter concluded that Guderian was an "ardent and unquestioning disciple of the Führer."[24] Indeed, Guderian employed the same divide and rule tactics that underpinned Hitler's method of leadership. He tried threats and rewards, friendship and hostility to bring pressure to bear on Hitler while simultaneously enhancing his own position, influence, and prestige within the inner circle of national socialism. He even attempted to influence Himmler. But Guderian left Göring, who disliked working, alone, perceiving him to be a waning star. This reflected his general disdain of the Luftwaffe and his underappreciation of the impact of air operations on ground warfare. He showed a particular lack of interest in the potent tank-busting tactical aviation that the Luftwaffe established during 1943.[25] Guderian undoubtedly believed, in his ego and vanity, that he was the man who might yet save Germany from the catastrophe into which Hitler and inept generals seemed to be leading her.[26]

Guderian went to Kursk and watched the offensive. Predictably, the new Panther tank failed through serious mechanical defects—the product of hasty procurement, production, and commitment without full trials and testing. Guderian viewed Kursk as the strategic turning point of the war—revealing how limited was his understanding of strategy—because of his perception that the panzer divisions he had reconstituted had been decisively defeated. But Guderian exaggerated the degree of damage done: we now know that German tank losses at Kursk were less than Guderian and others perceived at the time.[27]

After Kursk, Guderian allied himself with Speer and Zeitzler, chief of the General Staff, to launch a common strategy to minimize Hitler's influence by appointing someone else (i.e., Guderian) as army commander-in-chief. Secretive by nature, Guderian made these overtures unaware that both von Kluge and von Manstein had already proposed the idea of Hitler relinquishing the position to no avail. Again Guderian allowed his personal animosity toward von Kluge to prevent him from joining forces with the two generals who shared Guderian's objective, ensuring that his initiative was similarly rebuffed. His judgment of von Kluge as timid and incapable of standing up to Hitler precluded either reconciliation or cooperation.

The biggest obstacle to Guderian's forging an alliance with senior officers to circumscribe Hitler's control of operations was that he continuously politicked all those involved. While seeking out ways to diminish Hitler's power he strove to improve his own relations with leading Party officials in order to increase his influence with and access to the Führer. The commonly held view that Guderian was sympathetic to the Party (understandable as it was) hampered his efforts to rally opposition to Hitler. His unwillingness to resort to extrajudicial means (i.e., assassination), his lack of faith in the leading conspirators, and his well-developed sense of self-preservation guaranteed he could never be a leader of a conspiracy.

Unfortunately, Guderian's quest for power also hampered German efforts to enhance its defensive military capabilities when it desperately needed to do so in 1943. Germany's only remaining possible exit strategy would be to inflict such grievous losses on the enemy in grim attritional warfare that they abandoned their commitment to unconditional surrender and offered Germany better terms. Slim as the chances for success were, they represented the only viable strategy still open to Germany.

Moreover, his year away had left Guderian out of touch with the rapidly changing dynamics of mechanized warfare in Europe. On his return as Inspector General of Armored Troops, Guderian talked about recreating four-hundred-tank armored divisions—the kind of massed tank formations he had dreamed of before the war but which wartime experience had long taught were tank heavy. What Germany needed instead were more, better-balanced combined-arms formations of tanks, *Panzergrenadiers*, pioneers, and self-propelled artillery, antitank and antiaircraft guns, if Germany was to prevail in a grim, protracted attritional struggle.

During 1943 the strategic situation deteriorated further. The Axis lost its land bridge in North Africa, the Allies invaded Italy, Mussolini was deposed and then rescued and restored to a rump Fascist state. Germany's panzer forces were pushed firmly on the defensive and worn down in heavy attrition. Hitler's unwillingness to use the panzer forces' strategic mobility in defense compromised their effectiveness. Even so, under the strain of war, the German military was losing the mobility that had hitherto allowed it to evade destruction. Motor transport losses massively exceeded production and growing logistic problems saw mounting fuel supply difficulties.[28]

Guderian now came to stress offensive defense based on accurate battlefield intelligence. The woefully deficient nature of German human intelligence ensured that the German army relied heavily on aggressive battlefield reconnaissance for its tactical intelligence.[29] Guderian therefore tried to rehabilitate the armored reconnaissance units in order to enhance understanding of enemy dispositions, strengths, and intentions. Gradually (and grudgingly) he also came to see the unavoidable need for infantry formations to have their own organic antitank capability (though he instinctively opposed this diminution of armored concentration). He acceded to infantry receiving assault guns to delay enemy breakthrough forces, while armored reserves moved up to seal penetrations, repel the invaders, and restabilize the front in a defensive "fire brigade" role before being withdrawn for rest, refitting for their next emergency rescue mission. Already in 1942 infantry divisions were receiving newly improvised tank destroyers. During 1943 Guderian agreed to the diversion of assault guns from the artillery to the infantry because these resources would not decrease the armored force allotment. Yet, during 1943 he opposed the development of purpose-built tank destroyers (*Jagdpanzers*) intended for defensive infantry support, even though this type of vehicle would ultimately prove to be among the most formidable in the German armory.

His long institutional struggle with the artillery arm also kept him opposed to the provision of adequate mobile self-propelled artillery to support mechanized formations. The artillery of the panzer divisions remained largely motorized for the entire war, which weakened its ability to keep pace with and therefore participate in mobile offensive and defensive operations. Pushed increasingly on the defensive during 1942–3, the Germans relied ever more often on artillery fire support for their successes. These experiences illuminated the urgent need for self-propelled artillery weapons. Yet Germany had only two main self-propelled artillery pieces: the 105mm "Wasp" and the 150mm "Bumble Bee." Largely as a result of Guderian's insistence, these were produced only in limited numbers, sufficient at best to equip a single battalion in each panzer artillery regiment during 1943–5. The lack of self-propelled guns reflected Guderian's opposition to diverting resources and productive capacity to artillery weapons and his firm prewar belief that only tanks could fight other tanks effectively.[30] This was a mistake. Wartime experience proved that the combination of firepower and mobility (which made them difficult targets to neutralize) made self-propelled artillery powerful weapons in the German armored arsenal.

But the military situation prevented Guderian from making much headway in restoring combat power of the armored force during 1943. What success he had in increasing combat power came through the introduction of more formidable tank destroyers (which he remained lukewarm about), the ironing out of the major flaws in the third generation Panther and Tiger tanks, and general increased production. But these developments had all been in the works a long time (something that did not stop Guderian from typically trying to take personal credit for these accomplishments in his memoirs). He emphasized extensive gunnery practice, so that German tank gunners remained unmatched in terms of technical skill until the end of the war, aided by first-rate optics. On the defensive, German armored fighting vehicles inflicted a steadily rising toll on their enemy, but it was never enough to offset the enemy's substantial and increasing numerical superiority.

During 1943, the enemy's increasing domination of the skies began to impede the battlefield mobility of German armor, precipitating another heated debate on how to counter the enemy's tactical aviation. Guderian was no supporter of military aviation. In 1936 he had anticipated few opportunities for aircraft to cooperate with his vaunted armored forces.[31] The spring 1940 tactical training between Guderian's XIX Motorized Corps and the Luftwaffe Stukas of II Air Corps emerged as a result of a Luftwaffe initiative, not one of Guderian's.[32] Enemy air superiority led to increasing air attacks on German armored forces and lines of communications, which hampered and disrupted German movement and mechanized operations. Passive countermeasures—light and medium antiaircraft guns (either towed or mounted on half-tracks)—helped to minimize but could not neutralize this growing threat.

Guderian finally became concerned with this problem when he belatedly recognized that enemy air power was affecting the battlefield performance of his panzers. Thus he came to embrace a new armored fighting vehicle concept—the *Flakpanzer*—self-propelled antiaircraft guns mounted on a fully-tracked chassis—that emerged from the troops during the fall of 1943, and he supported a range of increasingly powerful improvised *Flakpanzers* through the end of the war.[33] Guderian authorized a *Flakpanzer* platoon (and during 1944 a company) for every panzer regiment.

In his memoirs Guderian emphasized the combative aspects of his relationship with Hitler. But the transcripts of Führer conferences Guderian attended reveal a different picture; most of the time Hitler and Guderian were in general agreement and cooperated effectively.[34] When they clashed, the cause was usually a disagreement over means, rather than ends. However, it is clear that the tension between them gradually increased over time. In January 1944 they had a major disagreement when Guderian pressed Hitler to build a major defensive system to cover Germany's eastern frontier. Again Guderian tried to get Hitler to nominate a single general he trusted to command military operations and once again failed. He concluded that increasingly Hitler looked to the SS and the Party for trusting supporters and that ultimately the SS would take charge of the army. His response to that trend was to more strongly identify himself and the armored troops with the national socialist worldview and agenda.

The anti-Hitler conspirators had kept peripheral contact with Guderian during 1943 but were no more successful than before in persuading him to act against his lawful commander-in-chief and sovereign head of state. In the spring of 1944, as Guderian clashed more frequently and violently with Hitler, they tried once again to draw him into the conspiracy. But one must remember the episodic and temporary nature of the Hitler–Guderian disagreements. Hitler still had faith in Guderian and vice versa.

That Guderian had become out of touch with strategic realities was reflected by his support of Geyr von Schweppenburg against Rommel in the bitter controversy that emerged during the fall of 1943 regarding the appropriate strategy for defending against possible invasion in the west. Guderian wanted to keep armored forces back in deep reserve for a massive, concentrated armored counteroffensive. Having far less personal experience than Rommel of the growing menace that Allied air power posed to the strategic, tactical, and operational mobility of armored forces, Guderian failed to perceive this new threat. He also failed to appreciate that the Allies' maritime mastery would allow their naval forces to inflict grievous damage on German mechanized forces trying to repel an invader back into the sea. Rommel, with more recent experience of growing Anglo-American combat power, had lobbied for the only strategy that offered even minimal prospects for success: immediate counterthrust by all available mechanized reserves to force the Allies back before they could consolidate their lodgment.

Guderian's strategic failings, therefore, contributed to Germany's failure to thwart the Allied Second Front during the summer of 1944. This failure coincided with equally grievous strategic defeats on the Eastern Front and Italy, defeats that finally galvanized the anti-Hitler opposition into action.

Guderian and the 20 July 1944 Conspiracy

G UDERIAN'S ACTIONS during the 20 July 1944 assassination attempt on Hitler bear special attention because they speak
volumes about Guderian's true character. To recap, it was in 1942–3
while he was unemployed and bitter that four members of the anti-
Hitler resistance—General Friedrich Olbricht, Dr. Carl Goerdeler,
Major General von Tresckow, and General Friedrich von Rabenau—
all made unsuccessful overtures to lure him into the conspiracy.[1] In
his postwar memoirs, Guderian freely acknowledged some of these
interactions; yet, although he became fully aware of the plot to remove Hitler, he did not denounce the conspirators. According to his
memoirs, he sympathized with them but concluded that the scheme
lacked sufficient prospects of success to hazard his career and life.[2]
He also offered patriotism and loyalty to the Prussian tradition as
reasons why he had refused to join the conspiracy—it was unfeasible
and would be hazardous to the national interests of Germany and
the German people.[3]

In late 1943 the assassination plot developed momentum under
the dynamic leadership of Colonel Claus Graf von Stauffenberg, and
a plan evolved. After Hitler's assassination, General Fromm would
use his authority as head of the Replacement Army to declare a state

of emergency and to order "Operation Valkyrie," the code word for emergency mobilizations of the Replacement Army to deal with enemy parachute landings or insurrections among slave workers or concentration camp inmates. This would give the conspirators a force of regular army troops who, while ignorant of the conspiracy, could be used by the conspirators to round up leading Nazi and SS commanders and help the plotters consolidate their power and authority.

Though they had failed in their earlier enlistment attempts and remained wary of Guderian and his relations with the Nazi leadership, the conspirators persisted in periodic efforts to enlist his support. Guderian would be a powerful ally for the new regime. Despite communicating with the conspirators through his deputy, Thomale (who had joined the conspiracy), Guderian again spurned new overtures they made in August 1943.[4] Fundamentally, Guderian's knowledge that his archenemy von Kluge was associated with the plot inevitably ruined any prospect of winning him over. However, according to Guderian's memoirs, he could not in good conscience murder a commander-in-chief to whom he had sworn an oath of allegiance; while, pragmatically, he felt the attempt doomed to failure anyway.[5]

Despite Guderian's *mea culpa*, there is strong circumstantial evidence to indicate that Guderian was more involved than he admits. For instance, it is intriguing that in early June 1944 Guderian recommended to Himmler that von Stauffenberg—the dynamo behind the conspiracy—become the army's chief of staff. If Hitler had acted on Guderian's recommendation this would have removed the greatest impediment to the assassination attempt—lack of direct access to Hitler. One must concur with Peter Padfield's conclusion that it is unlikely that Guderian at this stage was unaware of von Stauffenberg's leading role in the conspiracy.[6]

In July 1944, as the war went ever more disastrously on all fronts, the plotters finally launched their assassination attempt. On 18 July, as Guderian himself admitted in his memoirs, his former Luftwaffe liaison officer from Russia, von Barsewisch, who had developed and maintained a close relationship with Guderian, came to see him as an emissary of the conspirators in a final attempt to enlist Guderian's participation. Barsewisch informed Guderian of the impending attempt on Hitler's life, even though he did not say precisely when it would occur, as the final decision had not yet been made.[7] In his memoirs, Guderian disingenuously omitted any mention of this.[8] But von Barsewisch failed to convince Guderian, who continued to plead loyalty to his military oath. Nevertheless, he conveniently forgot his military duty when he neglected to report the planned assassination to the Führer. Clearly, Guderian was soliciting favor from both sides. In his memoirs he lamely says that he decided the information was too incredible to take seriously: a defense that borders on the preposterous![9]

The very next day, however, Guderian set out on a highly unusual unscheduled inspection of newly activating armored units of the Replacement Army. "Coincidently," these were some of the very units that Fromm intended to use, under cover of "Operation Valkyrie," to consolidate the new regime's power after Hitler's assassination. While visiting antitank troops at Allenstein, Thomale called Guderian to say that von Olbricht, now a chief conspirator, had requested a 24-hour delay in the departure of armored units from Berlin to the front in East Prussia, so that they could participate in an "Operation Valkyrie" mobilization rehearsal the following day. In his memoirs Guderian alleged that he initially demurred because these units were urgently needed to help rebuild a new defensive front after the Soviet summer offensive had destroyed the Army Group Center; every man and tank that could be scraped together had already been sent east for this purpose. Yet, Thomale (another conspirator) allegedly finally persuaded Guderian to delay the scheduled transfer of these units for a day or two, Guderian ultimately agreeing with the two conspirators that such a minimal delay would cause no harm.

There can hardly be any doubt that, with his keen intellect, Guderian clearly appreciated the role assigned to these armored units by the conspirators and that the 24-hour delay Olbricht requested indicated that the assassination attempt was at hand. Further, not only must he have known the day, but logically he must also have accurately discerned the precise timing of the assassination attempt. The pure mechanics of assassination required that the conspirators get close to Hitler, which would only be possible at the next Führer conference, scheduled (as they always were) for the afternoon of the 20th. If this is so, then his failure to arrest Barsewisch, Olbricht, and Thomale, or at least to denounce their imminent assassination plot, constituted nothing less than treason. Moreover, by agreeing to delay the transfer of these armored units, Guderian crossed the line he had been hovering over and effectively joined the 20 July 1944 assassination conspiracy, notwithstanding his attempts to cover his tracks lest things should go wrong.

Such a conclusion is strongly reinforced by Guderian's actions on 20 July. After his unusual inspection of troops for public consumption and to help provide him with a solid alibi if the coup failed, he traveled from Berlin to his Diepenhof estate in West Prussia. It is true that Guderian occasionally took time off to endulge in gentleman farming on his estate. But that mere coincidence had him retire to his estate—while crisis raged on the central Eastern Front—on the same afternoon that von Stauffenberg tried to assassinate Hitler beggars the imagination. It was a journey of some hours, and it required perfect timing to fit in an early morning inspection and then hasten to his estate prior to the start of the Führer conference. Guderian then ensured that he would be incommunicado at the time of the assassination attempt, hunting roebuck on his estate, alone. Guderian had learned this tactic some twenty-five years earlier from his former *Freikorps* commander, Rüdiger von der Goltz, who had gone off hunting when he wanted to avoid orders that he did not want to follow.[10]

It was late afternoon before a dispatch rider tracked down Guderian "innocently" wandering around his estate. Guderian had bought himself crucial time to see which way the plot had gone. When he heard over the radio that a failed bombing attempt had been made on the Führer's life, he immediately set about isolating himself from suspicion. In the meantime, his complicit deputy, Thomale, was working hard to cover his master's tracks and deflect the suspicion that did come his way. At midnight Thomale phoned and confirmed the plot had failed and that the lead conspirators were already dead or under arrest.

It was thus a combination of good fortune and prudence that saved Guderian from the fate that befell von Kluge and even Rommel, namely, disgrace and death. Now, in the failure of the conspiracy (and perhaps all along) Guderian saw an opportunity for himself to rise to a new task—of saving Germany from both its external enemies and Hitler.

Suspicion quickly, and correctly, fell on Guderian, as one of the panzer replacement units had received mobilization orders from Fromm and had dutifully headed toward Berlin in accordance with their preexisting orders. It refused the orders of Major Remer, the local army commander then engaged in crushing the revolt and proclaimed (quite correctly) that it took orders only from Guderian, as Inspector General of Armored Troops. Thus the plot almost unwittingly succeeded in ensnaring Guderian, albeit after the fact. At 6:00 p.m. Hitler asked General Thomale about Guderian's whereabouts, and an hour later Thomale had to answer further probing questions about Guderian's activities. With Thomale deftly covering, Guderian passed this initial scrutiny and Hitler, still dazed by the bomb attempt, elevated Guderian to the position of Acting Chief of the General Staff and ordered him to the Army High Command headquarters at Lötzen.

Why did Hitler do this? Guderian was immediately available to fill in this moment of immediate crisis. Moreover, the officer Hitler had intended for the vacant position (Zeitzler having taken sick leave several weeks earlier), Buhle, a more compliant man than Guderian, had been wounded by the bomb detonation and would not be fit for months at least. That Hitler was nonetheless suspicious of Guderian is reflected by his promoting Guderian only to the position of Acting Chief of the General Staff, as a temporary measure until Buhle's recovery. Hitler was wisely wary of Guderian's ambition, and he recalled the latter's 1943 efforts to reorganize the command structure and persuade Hitler to renounce supreme command.[11] Finally, it was widely known that Guderian's relationship with the Armed Forces High Command had long been acrimonious.[12]

Thus on 20 July 1944, Heinz Guderian reached the pinnacle of his military career through good fortune, cunning, and calculated political neutrality. Yet, there can be little doubt that if the conspirators had succeeded in assassinating Hitler and rallying the bulk of the armed forces to them that afternoon, Guderian would have emerged from his self-imposed seclusion on his country estate and proceeded wholeheartedly to support the new regime. It is also highly likely, given his character, that he would have demanded a significant promotion as reward for his support: for, Guderian was, after all, always both a survivor and an opportunist.

Guderian as Acting Chief of the General Staff, 1944–1945

I~N HIS~ memoirs Guderian claimed that he only took the appointment as Acting Chief of the General Staff because he was ordered to do so by Hitler and out of a patriotic duty in an effort to save German civilians from the vengeful Soviets.[1] However, in reality, events show that he had actively sought such a position of power and influence since 1941.

Yet, as Acting Chief of the Army General Staff, Guderian's duties were restricted to advising Hitler on the Eastern Front; all the other theaters remained the responsibility of the Armed Forces High Command. He did not resent this as he usually resented other restrictions, because the Eastern Front was the theater that mattered most to him. That this was the case can be seen in his abandonment of his predecessor Zeitzler's abortive efforts to redirect the other war theaters back under control of the Army High Command. In his new job Guderian repeatedly demonstrated his lack of supreme command ability by routinely denigrating both the strategic importance and the resource needs of the other theaters.[2] To Guderian, the war was the Eastern Front.

Guderian brought his typical impetuosity and vivacity to his new position. He spoke powerfully and bluntly (qualities Hitler liked), offending and alienating many within Hitler's inner circle, as he had done throughout his life. However, it soon became clear that Guderian's appointment could have no positive impact on the hopeless command relationships that bedeviled the Nazi High Command.[3] While he brought a greater degree of frankness to the daily Führer briefings, little practical benefit emerged, nor could it. Guderian proved no more successful in shaping Hitler's strategic decision making than any other of the senior German military commanders before him.

Guderian's disdain for the other services ensured that interservice friction escalated during his tenure as chief of staff.[4] In September Guderian got into a furious argument with Göring after trying to poach Luftwaffe trucks to restore the mobility of his shattered panzer divisions. Likewise, he made little progress in altering the existing allocation of service resources in the face of entrenched institutional defense of their existing missions and resources.[5]

Guderian nonetheless went about his job with energy and enthusiasm, confident that his military ability alone could conjure a miracle and somehow save a Germany that strategists knew was doomed to defeat. The burden and responsibility that confronted Guderian was enormous, and in reality, well beyond his capabilities since Germany's situation was irretrievable. He naively believed his skill could somehow still lay the preconditions for political negotiations that would generate peace terms that would preserve the German state.[6] This was the same political naiveté that Guderian had displayed at the end of the Great War.

In addition, Hitler made Guderian a member of the honor court that screened and discharged members of the armed forces accused of involvement in the 20 July conspiracy so that a specially convened people's court could convict them (after Gestapo torture) and execute them—by hanging by piano wire. In his memoirs, Guderian claimed he took this onerous mandate only with the greatest reluctance and in an effort to shield and save a least a few of the more peripherally involved conspirators.[7]

Yet, once again Guderian's true motives are questionable. Given his own suspicious involvement in the conspiracy, as well as the more overt involvement of his deputy, Thomale, Guderian had a motive (self-preservation) to influence the expeditious discharge of conspirators from the army. Certainly, his participation in the honor court makes questionable his claim to have been motivated by a desire to preserve the honor of the army. He voted to expel officers exclusively on the basis of Gestapo interrogation and intelligence reports, denying the defendants any opportunity to present a defense, testify, or even call witnesses (which of course might incriminate others). Such procedures blatantly violated the basic principles of German military justice that Guderian claimed to hold so dear. The "judges" did manage to salvage Rommel's chief of staff, Hans Speidel, who had covered his trail almost as well as Guderian. One could make the case that, if Guderian had allowed Speidel to be kicked out of the army, it would have been the thin end of the wedge, whereby other peripherally involved officers (i.e., those who had spurned the advances of the conspirators but not denounced them) might too be condemned. Again, the evidence allows one to surmise that it was naked self-preservation that saw Guderian fight to save just a handful of select officers from expulsion from the army.

Guderian also constantly fought encroachments on the power and influence of the army—from the SS, Luftwaffe, and the Armed Forces High Command, in particular—which gained momentum after the assassination attempt. The large-scale involvement of General Staff officers in the coup attempt saw unrelenting attacks by Hitler, Himmler, and the Armed Forces High Command to emasculate the General Staff. Yet, despite his elevation, Guderian actually had a long-standing bias against the General Staff, the very institution he now commanded. He held the quite false notion that the General Staff had opposed his attempts to introduce modern armored warfare principles during the 1930s.[8]

Forced on the defensive, Guderian backed Hitler and pushed the Nazification of the army and its general staff. On 29 July, Guderian issued an order requiring "all General Staff officers to be National Socialist officers."[9] He thus presided over the final and complete Nazification of the German army during the last year of the war. During this period, the Nazi salute became obligatory throughout the armed forces. It is interesting that Guderian mentioned neither

development in his memoirs.[10] In an address on 24 August he hypo-
critically described the 20 July plot as the "darkest day in the history of
the German General Staff."[11] Whether out of ideological commitment,
sheer pragmatism, or a desire to dispel lingering concerns about his
involvement in the conspiracy (most likely a combination of all three),
Guderian trumpeted Hitler's demands. By these substantial sacri-
fices to the honor of the army, Guderian dispelled any lingering doubt
about his involvement in the 20 July conspiracy and reingratiated
himself with Hitler, at least temporarily. Moreover, belying his claims
of reluctance, once installed, Guderian repeatedly asked Hitler to
make his appointment permanent; and it was at Guderian's personal
initiative that a National Socialist Leadership Officer joined his headquarters. While not ideologically a Nazi, he was prepared to do anything that might advance himself. In retrospect, his behavior can be
seen as overcompensation by a man with a guilty conscience. But,
apparently, he failed to see why other officers perceived him as a
"Nazi" when he choose to embrace the increased politicization of the
military as a necessary evil to buttress morale and fighting will.

During 1944 and 1945, Guderian came ever more to ape his
master. Both clung to the quixotic dream of a last minute reversal of
fortune. Guderian like his master clung to the shining example of
Frederick the Great, who had never abandoned his struggle despite
impending doom, and had survived the Seven Years' War. Both men
persistently hoped for a miraculous strategic victory that would allow Germany to fashion a semblance of an acceptable peace. As a
patriot he was naturally fearful of Soviet reprisals (which fully aware
of the heinous nature of German behavior in the east, he understood
would be vicious) and his deep-seated anticommunism made him
determined to continue the fight against the evils of Bolshevism. He
naively clung to the vain notion that a local success in the west would
allow Germany to achieve a separate peace. His exaggerated sense of
his ability and his attraction to national socialism left Guderian more
like his master than he dared recognize. In fact, one historian has
concluded that even at this late juncture, Guderian remained one of
Hitler's "most ardent admirers."[12] What is more, he shared Hitler's
and the Armed Forces High Command's "strategic myopia and the
same callous determination to fight to the last."[13]

Guderian's actions during the fall of 1944 contradict his postwar claims that he had become disillusioned with Hitler.[14] During August Guderian was confronted with the problem of the Warsaw Uprising and its brutal suppression, in which the German forces involved committed numerous atrocities. In his memoirs Guderian went to some length to distance himself from these war crimes and to accentuate his alleged efforts to mitigate the excesses of the SS and police. He did this, he claimed, because he viewed the atrocities as a stain on the army's reputation and honor, rather than because he believed the atrocities themselves to be immoral: the atrocities increased Polish resistance and tenacity when the rising had to be suppressed quickly to shore up the weak Eastern Front and halt the Soviet advance into his beloved Prussia. Guderian demanded that the city be declared part of the fighting front, so that it would come under army command, but Hitler refused, leaving SS Colonel General Erich von der Bach-Zelewski's antipartisan forces in control of the vicious suppression of the uprising. Although he was well aware of the merciless antipartisan war that German forces had been conducting in the east, this was the first time Guderian had been placed in a position where he had to deal with Nazi brutality directly. The suppression of the Warsaw uprising can have left Guderian in no doubt of the depravity of Hitler and the senior regime leadership. Nevertheless, he once again so deftly covered his tracks that he successfully avoided prosecution at Nuremberg. Yet, Guderian was neither prepared to resign nor to allow the excesses committed to damage his relationship with Hitler.

But over time the Guderian–Hitler relationship inevitably deteriorated. Guderian's squeamishness regarding the suppression of the Warsaw Uprising in fact disappointed Hitler—it was not a trait he expected from a true national socialist officer. During mid-August the pair had a major argument when Guderian blamed military failures on lack of air force and naval support, a frequent refrain of his. He also proved unable to prevent the Soviets from driving Army Group North back through the Baltic and isolating it in the Courland peninsula, essentially taking it out of the war. Nor was he able to prevent the collapse of Army Group North Ukraine or prevent the Red Army from penetrating the border of his beloved East Prussia in the fall. He was unable to mitigate the collapse of Army Group South Ukraine and the subsequent loss of Romania, which compelled the Germans to retreat from the Balkans.

During August 1944 Guderian pushed for a major defensive fortification effort along Germany's eastern frontier—the *Reichsschützstellung*—and the formation of new fortress troops by rigorous combout actions at home to man this defensive wall. Again, desire to save his precious Prussia largely motivated these initiatives. However, to Guderian's consternation, Hitler extended the idea to include the rehabilitation of the West Wall and the subsequent diversion of a substantial proportion of the fortress troops to the west. Despite his adamant opposition, these measures contributed directly to halting the Allied advance roughly along the German frontier by winter. Had Guderian had his way, the Allies might well have pushed through the Huertgen and approached the Rhine and the essential war industrial complex of the Ruhr before the end of 1944.

Similarly, Guderian strongly opposed the December 1944 Ardennes Offensive because of the grave threat he perceived in the east against his beloved East Prussia and family estate. In fact, he demonstrated far less concern about the vulnerability of the Ruhr, even though it was far more strategically vital to the German war effort, than he did for East Prussia. Ancestral loyalties thus overrode his previous hope of a dramatic reversal of fortune in the west from which Germany could negotiate peace with the western powers. He naively believed that the reserves committed to the Ardennes offensive were sufficient to turn back the Soviet steamroller in the east: they were not. At best, if Guderian had them at his disposal he might have slightly retarded the pace of the Soviet onslaught and marginally mitigated the calamity that was the German defeat on the Vistula River and the subsequent Soviet advance to the Oder River during the spring of 1945.

His obsession regarding the Eastern Front came to a head on 24 December when he appeared at the *Adlerhorst* (Hitler's field headquarters in the west) and tried hard to get Hitler to shift the German center of gravity back to the east. A vicious brawl ensued—Hitler was fixated on the illusory goal of recovering the initiative in the west and foolishly believed he had—and was in no mood to tangle with Guderian. It was a further proof of Guderian's waning career. Guderian failed completely, as Hitler dismissed as fabrication the most detailed intelligence estimates of overwhelming Soviet superiority. Guderian tried again on 31 December and 9 January to no avail. Subsequent events proved Guderian correct; yet anyone could see the impending calamity on the Eastern Front.

Likewise, Guderian was incensed when Hitler transferred the Sixth Panzer Army from the west in February not to the Oder front, but instead to Hungary. Guderian poorly understood the larger strategic picture—particularly the German war economy's critical dependence on the few remaining Hungarian oil fields.[15] Hitler was again right in fearing that the German war economy could not continue without the Hungarian oil, a larger strategic picture than Guderian was unable to comprehend. Despite his complaints, Guderian had only himself to blame. On 31 December 1944, he had sent a telex to the Hungarian High Command indicating that the relief of Budapest was Germany's highest priority. Guderian had taken to lying in a desperate effort to keep the Hungarians—now Germany's only remaining ally—in the war. Like his master, Guderian cloaked himself in an amazing veil of self-deception. [16]

He also resorted to ideological fanaticism in a flailing, last-ditch effort to enhance the German military's fighting abilities and powers of resistance. He enthusiastically supported the activation of the Home Guard (*Volkssturm*) under party leadership during the fall of 1944, and on 6 November, he told home guard troops that they would prove to the enemy that there were "85 million National Socialists who stand behind Adolf Hitler"[17] Yet his repeated efforts to usurp command of *Volkssturm* in threatened eastern Germany from the Nazi Party all proved abortive.[18]

As Acting Chief of the General Staff, Guderian continued his long-standing petty feud with Walter von Kluge. One of his first acts—within hours of being appointed acting CGS, in fact—was to seek von Kluge's removal as commander-in-chief west on the grounds that von Kluge was not a commander of armored forces.[19] His continued attacks on von Kluge's handling of the Mortain counteroffensive demonstrated that Guderian had no better grasp of the realities of combat on the Western Front than did Hitler. In 1944,

Guderian continued to think of and advocate the kind of large-scale maneuver operation of the Blitzkrieg heyday of 1941. This reveals that he was operationally as well as strategically out of touch with reality. His efforts came to no avail but fortunately for Guderian von Kluge's suicide in August 1944 (after coming under unfair suspicion for trying to make a separate peace in the west) must have delighted Guderian.

Guderian did on rare occasions, by dint of persistence and firm argumentation, succeed in at least modifying Hitler's demands and plans. During August he succeeded in switching reserves from the southern flank (Romania) to reinforce the northern flank (that closest to East Prussia), thus leaving Army Group South vulnerable to destruction later that month and compelling the Germans to retreat from the Balkans. He oversaw the brief opening of a corridor to the beleaguered German forces isolated in Courland, but Hitler refused to order an evacuation, the link was severed soon again and an entire army group was tied down defending this isolated enclave. Guderian believed that Courland held no strategic significance and he feared for the fate of the soldiers if they fell into Soviet hands. He repeatedly argued for a strategic withdrawal from Courland, a move Hitler opposed, and this dispute further damaged their relationship.

Guderian simultaneously remained Inspector General of Armored Troops (he adamantly refused to relinquish the position), but of course, of necessity, day-to-day control of the armored forces increasingly passed to his able deputy, Thomale. Together, they shepherded a series of formidable new armored fighting vehicles into service during the fall of 1944—the Tiger II heavy tank, the excellent Jagdpanzer IV/70 tank destroyer, and the formidable Jagdpanther. These new weapons and the continuing increase in armored production—which peaked in the late summer—only encouraged Hitler to resume the offensive in the west during the winter, when the impact of Allied aerial mastery would be lessened.

Guderian was careful to cultivate warm relationships with the most powerful men of the Third Reich who had access to Hitler. For example, he developed such a good working relationship with Reichsführer-SS Heinrich Himmler that Himmler invited Guderian to an exclusive dinner with him on Christmas Day 1944.[20]

Guderian ultimately came to realize that direct opposition to Hitler was largely unproductive. He turned to tried and tested alternatives, either ignoring Hitler's orders or trying to circumvent them. Such tactics occasionally succeeded.

It was during his visits to the front over the winter of 1944–5 that Guderian finally realized and accepted that the war was lost. The massive Soviet January offensive shattered the German defenses and proceeded to overrun East Prussia. Amazingly, his wife, Gretel, persisted in her efforts to run their estate until the last minute, when she fled and moved in with her husband at Zossen. Guderian despaired when Hitler chose the militarily inept Himmler to command a newly raised Army Group Vistula, tasked with restoring a new defensive front not on the Vistula (now long lost) but on the Oder before Berlin.

One of Guderian's most important military accomplishments in the last year of the war was his genesis of the successful February 1945 local counterattack that relieved the encircled garrison and inhabitants of Arnswalde. He wanted a spoiling attack (all that was possible) to throw the enemy off balance, successfully overrode Himmler's objections, and was assigned a competent General Staff officer—Wenck—to backstop the inexperienced Himmler and lead the strike. Launched on 16 February, it enjoyed initial success but suffered a major blow when Wenck was injured in a car accident. It accomplished only a little for a short while, nothing that could change Germany's strategic situation, which was irredeemable. This was the last battle Guderian was able to win.[21] But Guderian reaped strategic benefits out of all proportion to the limited tactical accomplishment achieved. The vigorous spoiling attack Guderian orchestrated instilled nervousness in the Soviet High Command (Stavka) about the vulnerability of its open northern flank before the Oder. Stavka thus decided to postpone the direct assault on Berlin until it had cleared this open flank in West Prussia and Eastern Pomerania during March 1945.[22] Guderian thus helped buy one month's respite for Berliners. It was probably his most notable achievement as Acting Chief of the General Staff.

In the spring of 1945 the disillusioned Guderian moved toward more overt political action. On 25 January, he tried to get Foreign

Minister von Ribbentrop to support him in pressing Hitler to request an armistice. During March, Guderian colluded with Speer when Hitler ordered a total scorched-earth policy leaving the aggressors nothing that they could use. Both recognized that this would have profound negative effects for the German people after the war. Guderian tried to limit the destruction of bridges and communications. In mid-March he visited Himmler and suggested that, because of his ill health, he might relinquish command to a more experienced field commander and then persuaded Hitler to replace him with a brilliant defensive improviser, Colonel-General Gotthard Heinrici, then in ascendancy after his distinguished defense of Silesia.

Von Ribbentrop took up Guderian's suggestion and secretly sent out feelers for a possible peace agreement. On 21 March, Guderian tried to co-opt Himmler to this plan, but Himmler rebuffed him. Triggered by Guderian's initiative, Himmler sent his own secret peace feelers to the west. Jodl also joined Guderian in dissuading the Führer from abrogating the Geneva Convention in March 1945; it would be one of his last accomplishments.

Yet even as late as 6 March 1945, Guderian participated in a propaganda broadcast denying the existence of the extermination camps that the Soviets had liberated. He proclaimed, "I have fought in the Soviet Union and have never seen gas chambers." The wording of this answer allowed him to maintain a technical honesty. Yet it is impossible to believe that someone as high ranking as Guderian did not know about death camps, since he regularly toured armored production facilities that routinely used slave labor drawn from the camp system.[23] Even Macksey concedes that in his position "Guderian must have known something about the death camps."[24]

During March, Guderian insisted on launching a counterattack to rescue the isolated garrison of Küstrin. Guderian shouted down Heinrici's objections that relief was impossible in precisely the same way that Hitler shouted down Guderian's opposition. So the offensive went ahead and inevitably failed. Guderian defended the decision, saying that everything that could be done to relieve the fortress had in fact been done: the enemy was too strong. Hitler denounced the preparations and enacting of the attack as negligent, something Guderian angrily refuted. Once again Guderian demonstrated "exemplary moral courage" in defending General Busse, the Ninth Army commander who had led the failed attack.[25] Guderian had fiercely defended his subordinates against higher authority throughout his career and this trait would contribute to his undoing. This was the final showdown: Hitler insisted that Guderian take six weeks "convalescent" leave effective immediately.

Guderian had tried to keep the army intact—remembering how a lack of an army had undermined efforts to make peace in 1919. In doing so, he had been forced to engage in politics. But Germany always came before his own person. He and Gretel retired to Munich, where he underwent heart treatment. Incredibly, on 1 May 1945— a week before the end of the war—he dutifully returned from his six weeks convalescent leave and rejoined his Inspector General of Armored Troops headquarters, which had in the meantime evacuated to the Tyrol, and reassumed his responsibilities. On 10 May 1945, he entered American captivity.

Why did Guderian soldier on under Hitler? One major reason was financial benefit. He continued to receive large-scale monthly bribes that massively increased his income until the end of the war. With his estate lost in Poland, he needed new accommodations and became more dependent than ever on these lucrative bribes. Even when sent on sick leave he continued to receive these payments and, in one last futile gesture, those senior officers remaining received a double bonus on 1 May 1945, the day after Hitler committed suicide in Berlin.[26] It is this double bonus that, perhaps, explains why Guderian bothered to return to a lost post that same day.

Guderian's Fate and Legacy

T HE YEAR 1945 witnessed a sudden and profound trans-
formation in Guderian's life. He went from Acting Chief of the General Staff to unemployed, to fugitive, to U.S. prisoner of war under
threat of prosecution for war crimes. He underwent interrogation
and—always the survivor—pragmatically cooperated with the Allies. Then, after charges of war crimes against him were dropped, he
wrote a series of evaluations for the U.S. Army Historical Division.[1]
These reports reflect the pride, arrogance, prejudice, insight, and
caustic wit that defined his persona. In them Guderian maintained
his animosity against old comrades, such as Halder and von Kluge.
Ever the pragmatist he told the Allies what they wanted to hear,
distancing himself from Hitler and the regime, emphasizing his professionalism and disdain for Nazism. In his secretly bugged cell,
however, he spoke with other senior officers about his admiration
for Hitler and national socialism and his contempt for the Allies,
admitting that the "basic principles of National Socialism had been
fine."[2]

In an example of the animus many German officers felt toward him, during 1948 Fabian von Schlabrendorff in his memoirs

accused Guderian of betraying the plotters in order to become Chief of Staff. Guderian threatened to sue for libel and forced the author to delete such comments in subsequent editions since von Schlabrendorff could not substantiate his allegations to the degree of proof required in a legal action.[3]

Likewise, Guderian evaded being tried as a war criminal at Nuremberg because at the time there was no substantial documentary or eyewitness testimony against him and there existed many other more easily prosecutable war criminals in Nazi Germany. His willingness to inform on his ex-colleagues and his general cooperativeness in answering the numerous questions the Allies asked him surely also helped him evade prosecution. He was, therefore, ultimately released and moved to a small house in Schwangau where he wrote his memoirs. These were published in 1951 and when translated into English the following year under the title *Panzer Leader* became a best-seller both in the United States and United Kingdom. Of course, Guderian was fortunate that most of the people in a position to challenge the accuracy of the claims made in his memoirs had already died during the war or been executed at Nuremberg.

Guderian remained an ardent and outspoken German nationalist until his death, arguing for German reunification as the Cold War evolved and for the need to revive the German military to confront the communist threat. It was a theme he had emphasized often during his life. However, Guderian himself would not live to see such efforts; he descended into ill health and died on 17 May 1954.

What can one make of Heinz Guderian? He was undoubtedly a maverick, an outsider who repeatedly flaunted rules or reinvented them. He was a man of progressive ideas and an able administrator capable of turning dreams into reality. Yet, he was an arrogant, ambitious egotist; he suffered from strategic myopia, a stubborn belief that he was always right, and was a political neophyte. His memoirs allowed him to carve out for himself an exaggerated role as the father of the German armored force that briefly wrought havoc across Europe during the halcyon years of Blitzkrieg, 1939–41.

Subsequent biographers have all too often uncritically embraced Guderian's self-image, so that Kenneth Macksey could conclude about him that "no other general in World War Two managed to impress so

wide and intrinsic a change upon the military art in so short a time."[4]
This biography contends that such eulogistic assertions inflate
Guderian's true accomplishments. Macksey claims that Guderian had
strategic insight, but in reality he was as woefully blinded to strategic
realities as Hitler and the rest of the senior German commanders.[5]

Guderian certainly had several great operational accomplishments—his strike deep into the Polish rear in September 1939; his
dash to the Channel in May 1940, splitting the Allies; his advance to
Smolensk and to Kiev during the summer of 1941. Macksey includes the halting of the Soviet steamroller before Warsaw in September 1944.[6] Guderian temporarily pushed a corridor through to
encircled Army Group North in August 1944. Yet, actually, his greatest
operational success as acting Chief of Staff was probably his last: the
spoiling attack he orchestrated during February 1945 into the open
northern flank of the Soviet advance on Berlin, which threw the
enemy off stride and allowed Berlin a precious extra month before
the final Soviet onslaught.

But most of his great successes were accomplished in positions of
substantial strategic, operational, and tactical advantage. Never was
he able to accomplish a lasting victory in a position of significant
disadvantage. He was a good tactician and technician: he firmly believed in the possibility of armor penetrating the Ardennes 1940; he
helped devise the communications and logistic infrastructures that
made Blitzkrieg warfare possible. He was progressive as well as inno-
vative, a creative trainer and instructor who demanded excellence
from his subordinates and proved a hard taskmaster. He was a charismatic, dynamic leader of men who achieved the best performance
out of his troops. He was a skillful administrator who repeatedly
juggled inadequate resources to accomplish significant tactical
deeds. He was a bold, daring commander who saw the strategic future for armored forces but who remained obsessed both with armor
(at the expense of truly combined-arms mechanized forces) and with
the inherent superiority of maneuver. Yet, he led too much from the
front, which hampered the smooth functioning of his headquarters.
He was impetuous, liable to react and act instinctively, sometimes
without thinking. He was overly optimistic and too determined to
have his way. He was undoubtedly a strong, charismatic personality

that drove himself very hard. He was a great organizer, an intellect, a theorist, and a technician.

But, in the final accounting, his deficiencies outweighed his strengths and he contributed directly to Germany's defeat. He bore considerable responsibility for the final abortive push on Moscow in December 1941; he proved unable to master that winter's defensive crisis. But his greatest weakness was his limited strategic understanding, which was probably worse than Hitler's: he remained fixated with the Eastern Front and gave scant due to the strategic requirements of the other theaters. He was an army man (and exclusively an armor man at that) who disdained interarms and interservice cooperation and coordination, with disastrous consequences. His ego and unswerving advancement of his beloved panzer force engendered enormous personal animus and accentuated institutional rivalries and conflicts.

He was actually little more successful than the other German generals in his dealings with Hitler. He was politically naive, believing that the army could control Hitler in the 1930s, and he never understood the Führer's true nature.[7] A genuine empathy existed between Guderian and his Führer and for far too long Guderian had believed that Hitler was Germany's savior. In fact, he came very late to perceive the menace and evil that was Hitler. For Guderian chose to believe that it was incompetent officers surrounding Hitler that dragged the Führer down and led him to make unwise decisions. Even when he finally realized that Hitler was leading the German people to their doom, in his arrogance Guderian believed that his genius and military abilities could save Germany. He tried for a long time to "educate" a megalomaniac, but inevitably failed. Only after 1942 did Guderian slowly begin to recognize Hitler's failings, and he lacked the courage to commit himself fully to the removal of Hitler. He remained uncommitted and was complicit in the 20 July 1944 assassination plot but covered his tracks artfully and emerged from its aftermath to a position of authority and prestige that in any other circumstances he could not have reached.

He never possessed innate political judgment and never saw the dangers in Nazism.[8] Instead, he admired Hitler's strength and embraced his hatred of communism. He remained far too trusting of

Hitler for far too long. He never understood national socialism in political terms. He was willing to challenge military matters that offended him but proved quite unwilling to challenge Hitler's political views because, one has to conclude, he generally concurred with them and embraced them. He was a committed anticommunist, an ardent nationalist, and a virulent militarist who empathized with much of the Nazi pathos. As time went by, his ego and ambition drew him ever closer to Hitler, the Party, and its leadership.

Guderian's biggest failing was his arrogance, which hampered the German war machine at every stage: in developing an armored force in the 1930s, in exacerbating the scale of defeat during winter 1941, and in the last year of the war when Guderian had very little military influence over Hitler or the war and no political influence over them. Nonetheless, he vainly continued—stubborn, arrogant, and tirelessly devoted to the end.

Notes

Introduction

1. Heinz Guderian, *Erinnerungen eines Soldaten* (Heidelburg: Kurt Vowinckel Verlag, 1951); translated in English as *Panzer Leader* (London: Michael Joseph, 1952).

2. Major biographies include Malte Plattenburg, *Guderian: Hintergründe des deutschen Schicksals, 1918–1945* (Düsseldorf: Abz-Verlag, 1950); John Keegan, *Guderian* (New York: Ballentine Books, 1973); Kenneth Macksey, *Guderian: Panzer General* (London: MacDonald and Jane's, 1975); Karl J. Walde, *Guderian: Ein Biographie* (Ullstein: Taschenbuch, 1976); Kenneth Macksey, *Guderian: Creator of the Blitzkrieg* (New York: Stein and Day, 1976); Dermot Bradley, *Generaloberst Heinz Guderian und den Entstehungsgeschichte des modernen Blitzkrieges* (Osnabrück: Biblio Verlag, 1978); Fred Frank, *Heinz Guderian: Beruhtester Panzerführer des II. Weltkrieges* (Rastatt: Pabel, 1985).

Chapter 1

1. Macksey, *Creator of the Blitzkrieg*, 23.
2. Ibid.
3. Macksey, *Panzer General* (London: Greenhill, 1997), 5–6.
4. Ibid., 6–7.
5. Ibid., 9–10.

Chapter 2

1. Macksey, *Panzer General*, 11–12.
2. Ibid., 14–15.
3. Ibid., 15.
4. Ibid., 16.
5. Ibid., 16.
6. Ibid., 17.

7. Timothy Lupfer, *The Dynamics of Doctrine: The Development of German Defensive Doctrine During the Great War* (Fort Leavenworth: U.S. Army Command and General Staff College Combat Studies Institute, 1981).
8. Macksey, *Panzer General,* 18.
9. Ibid.
10. For the training failures of German staff officers, see Trevor N. Dupuy, *A Genius for War: The German Army and General Staff, 1807–1945* (Englewood Cliffs, NJ: Prentice-Hall, 1977).
11. Bruce I. Gudmundsson, *Stormtroop Tactics: Innovation in the German Army, 1914–1918* (New York: Praeger, 1989); David T. Zabecki, *Steel Wind: Colonel Georg Brüchmüller and the Birth of Modern Artillery* (Westport, CT: Greenwood Press, 1995).
12. Macksey, *Panzer General*, 18–19.
13. Ibid., 20.
14. Ibid., 22.

Chapter 3
1. On the German collapse in the fall of 1918, see Ralph Lutz, ed., *Causes of the German Collapse in 1918* (Stanford, CA: Stanford University Press, 1934); John Wheeler-Bennett, *The Nemesis of Power* (London: Macmillan, 1964), part 1; and Rod Paschall, *The Defeat of Imperial Germany, 1917–18* (Chapel Hill, NC: Algonquin, 1989).
2. Macksey, *Panzer General*, 23.
3. Paschall, *Imperial Germany*, passim.
4. On the history of the Freikorps, see Nigel H. Jones, *A Brief History of the Birth of the Nazis: How the Freikorps Blazed the Trail for Hitler* (New York: Carroll and Graf, 2004); Robert Thoms and Stefan Pochanke, *Handbuch zur Geschichte der deutschen Freikorps* (Bad Soden-Salmünster: MTM-Verlag, 1997).
5. On the military and political failures of Imperial Germany, see among others, Fritz Fisher, *War of Illusions: German Policies from 1911 to 1914* (London: Chatto and Windus, 1975); Robert Asprey, *The German High Command at War* (New York: William Morrow and Co., 1991); Holger Herwig, "The Dynamics of Necessity: German Military Policy During the First World War," in Allan R. Millett and Williamson Murray, eds., *Military Effectiveness : The First World War* (Boston: Allen and Unwin, 1988), 1:80–115.
6. Hagen Schulze, *Freikorps und Republic, 1918–1920* (Boppard

am Rhein: H. Boldt, 1969), chapter 1.

7. Josef Bischoff, *Die Letzte Front: Geschichte der Eisernen Division im Baltikum, 1919* (Berlin: Schüzten Verlag, 1935), 37–9.

8. Vejas Liulevicius, *War Land on the Eastern Front: Culture, National Identity, and German Occupation in World War I* (Cambridge: Cambridge University Press, 2000).

9. Guderian, *Panzer Leader*, (New York: Ballentine, 1957), 7.

10. Macksey, *Panzer General*, 29.

11. Bischoff, *Letzte Front*, 192–202.

12. Macksey, *Panzer General*, 32.

13. Guderian's sole mention of these events in his memoir is a single line so cryptic as to be disingenuous: " . . . my departure from the Baltic had been in circumstances not of the happiest." Guderian, *Panzer Leader*, 7.

14. Dermot Bradley, *Generale des Heeres* (Osnabrück: Biblio Verlag, 1993), 4:472–4.

15. Macksey, *Panzer General*, 34.

16. Guderian, *Panzer Leader*, 7–8.

17. Macksey, *Panzer General*, 38.

18. Ibid., 52.

19. Ibid., 38.

20. Guderian, *Panzer Leader*, 8–10.

21. Macksey, *Panzer General*, 9.

22. Robert Citino, *The Path to Blitzkrieg: Doctrine and Training in the German Army, 1920–1939* (Boulder, CO: Lynne Rienner, 1999), 201.

23. James Corum, *The Roots of Blitzkrieg: Hans von Seeckt and German Military Reform* (Lawrence: University Press of Kansas, 1992), 139.

24. Citino, *Path to Blitzkrieg*, 201–202, 218n4.

25. W. Heinemann, "The Development of German Armoured Forces, 1918–40," in J. P. Harris and F. N. Toase, eds., *Armoured Warfare* (London: Batsford, 1990), 533.

26. Macksey, *Panzer General*, 43.

27. Citino, *Path to Blitzkrieg*, passim; Corum, *Roots of Blitzkrieg*, passim.

28. Macksey, *Panzer General*, 45.

29. Ibid., 47.

30. Guderian, *Panzer Leader*, 12–13.

31. Corum, *Roots of Blitzkrieg*, 130–36

32. Ibid., 134–36.
33. Ibid., 136.
34. Citino, *Path to Blitzkrieg*, 202.
35. Ibid.
36. This team also included Wilhelm Ritter von Thoma, who had helped suppress Hitler's 1923 Beer Hall Putsch using the 7th Motor Transport Battalion. Corum, *Roots of Blitzkrieg*, 137; U.S. Army, Military History Institute, Carlisle Barracks, PA, service record of General der Panzertruppen Ritter von Thoma.

Chapter 4
1. Corum, *The Roots of Blitzkrieg*; Citino, *Path to Blitzkrieg*.
2. Jehuda Wallach, *Dogma of the Battle of Annihilation* (Westport, CT: Greenwood Press, 1986); Azar Gat, *British Armour Theory and the Rise of the Panzer Arm: Revising the Revisionists* (London: Palgrove Macmillan, 2000).
3. Bradley, *Die Generale*, 4:474.
4. Corum, *Roots of Blitzkrieg*, passim; Citino, *Path to Blitzkrieg*, passim.
5. Macksey, *Panzer General*, 49.
6. Citino, *Path to Blitzkrieg*, 202–3.
7. Col. Lutz Oswald, "Anregungen und Lehren aus dem unter Leitung der Inspektion der Kraftfahrtruppen abgehaltened übungen der Kampfwagen-Nachildungs-Bataillone zusammen mit Infanterie und Artillerie auf den Truppenübungplätzen Grafenwöhr und Jüterbog," (Sept. 1932) microfilm series T-78, roll 300, frames 6250579–95, National Archives and Records Administration, Washington, DC.
8. The 7th Motor Transport Battalion, for example, was engaged in trials with motorcycle units as early as March 1924. U.S. Army Military History Institute, Carlisle Barracks, PA, service record of Wilhelm Josef Ritter von Thoma.
9. Macksey, *Panzer General*, 51.
10. Citino, *Path to Blitzkrieg*, 208–12.
11. Citino, *Path to Blitzkrieg*, 213–14.
12. Guderian, *Panzer Leader*, 18–19.
13. Macksey, *Panzer General*, 53.
14. It had sixteen clandestinely titled "tractor" tanks. Thomas J. Lentz, *Panzer Truppen: The Complete Guide to the Creation and Combat Employment of Germany's Tank Force, 1933–1942* (Atglen,

PA: Schiffer, 1996), 1:11.

15. Guderian, *Panzer Leader*, 39.

16. Williamson Murray, *The Change in the European Balance of Power, 1938–1939: The Path to Ruin* (Princeton, NJ: Princeton University Press, 1984), 37–8, 362. On the impact of Nazi propaganda in inflating British perceptions of German military strength, see Wesley Wark, *The Ultimate Enemy: British Intelligence and Nazi Germany, 1933–1939* (Ithaca, NY: Cornell University Press, 1985).

17. Williamson Murray, "German Military Effectiveness between 1919 and 1939," in Williamson Murray and Allan R. Millett, eds., *Military Effectiveness* (Boston: Unwin Hymen, 1988), 2:229–35.

18. Citino, *Path of Blitzkrieg*, 8–9.

19. Corum, *Roots of Blitzkrieg*, passim; Citino, *Path of Blitzkrieg*, chapters 2 and 3.

20. Macksey, *Panzer General*, 61.

21. Louis Lochner, ed., *The Goebbels Diaries, 1942–1943* (New York: Doubleday, 1948), 279.

22. Walther K. Nehring, *Panzerwaffe: die Geschichte der deutschen Panzerwaffe 1916 bis 1945* (Berlin: Propylaen, 1969), 88–9.

23. For a good summary of the inaccuracy of Guderian's interpretation of the struggle as progressives vs. reactionaries, see Corum, *Roots of Blitzkrieg*, 140–41.

24. Guderian, *Panzer Leader*, 21–2.

25. Wilhelm Deist et al., *Germany and the Second World War* (Oxford: Clarendon Press, 1990), 1:436.

26. Citino, *Roots of Blitzkrieg*, 230.

27. Deist, *Germany and the Second World War*, 1:434–6. On the Beck-Guderian controversy, see Hubertus Senff, *Die Entwicklung der Panzerwaffe im deutschen Heer zwischen den beiden Weltkriegen: Eine Untersuchung der Auffassungen über ihre Einsatz an Hand von Vorschriften, Literatischer Diskusssion und tatsächlichen Heeresaufbau* (Frankfurt am Main, 1969), 18ff.

28. Bradley, *Die Generale*, vols. 1–6, passim.

29. Citino, *Path to Blitzkrieg*, 212–15.

30. Jentz, *Panzer Truppen*, 11.

31. Macksey, *Panzer General*, 62.

32. Peter Chamberlain and Hilary Doyle, *Encyclopedia of German Tanks of World War Two* (London: Arms & Armour Press, 1999), 146.

33. Citino, *Path to Blitzkrieg*, 213.
34. Jentz, *Panzer Truppen*, 1:14–18.
35. Burkhart Müller-Hillebrand, *Das Heer, 1933–1945* (Darmstadt, E. S. Mittler u. Sohn, 1954), 1:25.
36. Deist, et al., *Germany in the Second World War*, 1:434–6.
37. Maximilian von Weichs and Generalleutnant Ernst Fessmann. Bradley, *Die Generale*, 4:453.
38. Only 333 tanks existed as of that date. Jentz, *Panzer Truppen*, 1:11–16.
39. Stephen Lewis, *Forgotten Legions: The Development of German Infantry Policy, 1918–1941* (New York, Praeger, 1973), passim.
40. Guderian, *Panzer Leader*, 26.
41. Walter Spielberger, *Sturmgeschütz and its Variants* (Atglen, PA: Schiffer, 1993), 10–20.
42. Jentz, *Panzer Truppen*, 1:15.
43. Wolfgang Fleischer, *Die deutschen Sturmgeschütze, 1935–1945* (Wölfersheim-Berstadt: Podzun-Pallas, 1996), 9–14.
44. Alexander Lassner, "The Invasion of Austria in March 1938: Blitzkrieg or Pfusch?" in Günter Bishof and Anton Pelinka, eds., *Contemporary Austrian Studies* (Piscataway, NJ: Transaction Publications, 2000), 447–87.
45. Guderian relied heavily on von Eimannsberger's *Der Kampfwagenkrieg* (1934). Corum, *Roots of Blitzkrieg*, 139. An excellent translation of Guderian's work is Chris Duffy's, published by Cassell and Co., London, 1992.
46. Murray, *European Balance of Power*; Richard Overy, *War and Economy in the Third Reich* (Oxford: Clarendon Press, 1994).
47. Guderian, *Panzer Leader*, 28–9.
48. Ibid., 30–36.
49. Lassner, "Invasion of Austria," 447–87.
50. Oberbefehlshaber der Heeresgruppen-kommando 3, "Bericht über den Einsatz der 8. Armeeoberkommando im März 1938," H. Gr. Kdo. 3 Stab, Dresden, 18 Juli 1939, microfilm series T-79, roll 14, frame 000447ff, National Archives and Records Administration, Washington, DC.
51. The division was short 15 percent of its combat strength when it reached the Austrian frontier, and one-third of its tanks were driven by drivers who had never driven tanks before. Lassner, "Invasion of Austria," 448–54.
52. Generalkommando Wehrkreis XIII, "Erfahrungsbericht über den Einsatz Österreich," microfilm series T-79, roll 274, 000948ff,

National Archives and Records Administration, Washington, DC.

53. T-79, 274, 000948ff.

54. Lassner, "Invasion of Austria," 456–59.

55. Ibid., 452.

56. Officially the 2d Panzer Division recorded a 17 percent breakdown rate during the anschluss. However, the evidence suggests that the records understated the real figures. Many tanks immobilized for want of fuel were omitted from these statistics. Erwin Schmidl, *März 38. Der deutsche Einmarsch in Österreich* (Vienna: Verlag der Österreichischen Staatsdruckerei, 1987), 153; Murray, *European Balance of Power*, 148.

57. Lassner, "Invasion of Austria," 461.

58. Ibid., 463–8.

59. Charles Messenger, *Sepp Dietrich: Hitler's Gladiator* (London: Brassey's, 1988), 68–9.

60. Lassner, "Invasion of Austria," 458.

61. Raymond Proctor, *Hitler's Luftwaffe in the Spanish Civil War* (Westport, CT: Greenwood Press, 1983); James Corum, "The Luftwaffe and the Coalition Air War in Spain, 1936–1939," *Journal of Strategic Studies* 18 (March 1995), 68–90.

62. Macksey, *Panzer General*, 74.

63. Telford Taylor, *Munich: The Price of Peace* (New York: Random House, 1979); Christopher Thorne, *The Coming of World War Two* (New York: Putnam, 1981).

64. Macksey, *Panzer General*, 77–8.

Chapter 5

1. Heinz Guderian, *Achtung! Panzer!* (Berlin: Offene Worte, 1936).

2. Macksey, *Creator of the Blitzkrieg*, 105. For information on Guderian's role in the campaign, see Robert Kennedy, *The German Campaign in Poland, 1939* (Washington, DC: Dept. of the Army, 1956), 79–85, 100–108; Guderian, *Panzer Leader*, 46–63.

3. Wallach, *Battle of Annihilation*.

4. Guderian fielded just 391 of the 2689 German tanks committed on 1 September 1939. Jentz, *Panzer Truppen*, 1:90–91.

5. These were the 1st–5th Panzer Divisions and the Panzer Formation Kempf constituted from the mobilized elements of the incomplete 10th Panzer Division. Jentz, *Panzer Truppen*, 1:92.

6. Guderian, *Panzer Leader*, 49.

7. Ibid.

8.   Steven Zaloga and Victor Madej, *The Polish Campaign 1939* (New York: Hippocrene Books, 1991), 110.

9.   Guderian, *Panzer Leader*, 50–52.

10. James V. Koch, review of Macksey, *Guderian: Panzer General* published by *H-German@h-net.msu.edu*, August 2003, 2. Available at www.h-net.org/reviews/showrev.egi?path=325991062538489.

11. Zaloga and Madej, *Polish Campaign*, 117–18.

12. Kennedy, *Poland*, 114–15.

13. Ibid., 95–6.

14. Guderian, *Panzer Leader*, 59–60.

15. Macksey, *Panzer General*, 88–9.

16. Kennedy, *Polish Campaign*, 96.

17. Macksey, *Creator of the Blitzkrieg*, 111–15.

18. Bradley, *Generaloberst Guderian*, 219.

19. Klaus Gerbet, ed., *Generalfeldmarshal Fedor von Bock: The War Diary, 1939–1945* (Atglen, PA.: Schiffer, 2000), passim.

20. Guderian, *Panzer Leader*, 62.

21. Zaloga and Madej, *Polish Campaign*, 155–6.

22. Macksey, *Creator of the Blitzkrieg*, 115.

23. Oberkommando des Heeres, *Kampferlebnisse auf Polen* (Berlin: Offene Worte, 1940), passim; Williamson Murray, "German Response to Victory in Poland: A Case Study in Professionalism," *Armed Forces and Society* 7, no. 2. (Winter 1981), 285–98.

24. Seventeen percent of all German tanks requiring factory overhaul served in Guderian's corps. Jentz, *Panzer Truppen*, 1:104.

25. "Erfahrungen beim Marsch motorisierter Verbände während des Feldzuges in Polen," Anl. 1 zu Erfahrungsbericht d. XV A.K, microfilm series T-312, roll 37, 7545415ff, National Archives and Records Administration, Washington, DC.

26. Charles Sydnor, *Soldiers of Destruction: The SS Death's Head Division, 1933–1945* (Princeton, NJ: Princeton University Press, 1977); Alexander Rossino, *Hitler Strikes Poland: Blitzkrieg, Ideology, and Atrocity* (Lawrence: University of Kansas Press, 2003); Christopher Browning, *Ordinary Men: Reserve Police Battalion 101 and the Final Solution in Poland* (New York: HarperCollins, 1992).

27. Macksey, *Creator of the Blitzkrieg*, 115.

28. Richard Giziowski, *The Enigma of General Blaskowitz* (London: Leo Cooper, 1997), chapters 7–8.

29. Macksey, *Creator of the Blitzkrieg*, 116.

30. From the National Archives and Records Administration, Washington, DC: 2 Lei. Div., "Erfahrungen bei den Operationen im Osten," Ia Nr. 393/39, 19.10.1939, microfilm series T-315, roll 436, frame 000480; XV A.K., "Erfahrungen auf taktischen Gebiet," 3.10.1939, microfilm series T-314, roll 550, frame 000295ff; XV A. K. "Der Feldzug in Polen," KTB XV A.K. Okt. 1939, microfilm series T-314, roll 550, frame 000222ff; OKH/ GenStdH O.Qu. I/Ausb. Abt. (Ia), "Taktisches Erfahrungen im polnischen Feldzug," 15.10.1939, microfilm series T-315, roll 436, frame 000462; Kennedy, *Poland*, 132–5; Murray, "German Response," 285–98.

31. Murray, "German Response," 285–98.

32. Macksey, *Panzer General*, 98.

33. Jentz, *Panzer Truppen*, 1:120–21.

34. Murray, "German Response," 285–98.

35. Robert Doughty, *The Seeds of Disaster: The Development of French Doctrine, 1919–1939* (Hamden, CT: Archon Books, 1985).

36. Florian Rothbrust, *Guderian's XIX Corps and the Battle of France* (Westport, CT: Praeger, 1990), chapters 1–2.

37. Sydnor, *Soldiers of Destruction*, 95–7.

38. Guderian, *Panzer Leader*, 97–8. On his rejection of a final armored assault see Macksey, *Creator of the Blitzkrieg*, 145–46.

39. Macksey, *Panzer General*, 123.

40. Ibid., 125.

41. On Rommel's military career in Africa see Desmond Young, *Rommel: the Desert Fox* (New York: Harper & Row, 1950).

42. Guderian, *Panzer Leader*, 117–18.

43. Ibid., 118–19.

Chapter 6

1. Guderian, *Panzer Leader*, 114.

2. R.H.S. Stolfi, "Equipment for Victory in France in 1940," *History*, 52, no. 183 (February 1970), 1–20.

3. Thomas Jentz, *Panzer Truppen*, 1:188–93.

4. Guderian, *Panzer Leader*, 117–18.

5. Ibid., 121–2.

6. Macksey, *Panzer General*, 130.

7. Omer Bartov, *Hitler's Army: Soldiers, Nazis and War in the Third Reich* (New York: Oxford University Press, 1993), 137–8.

8. See, among others, Hannes Heer and Klaus Naumann, eds.,

Vernichtungskrieg: Verbrechen der Wehrmacht, 1941–1944 (Hamburg: Hamburger Edition, 1995).

9. Oberkommando des Heeres, *Kampferlebnis auf Polen*; Allan Chew, *Fighting in the Russian Winter: Three Case Studies* (Fort Leavenworth: U.S. Army Command and General Staff College, 1981); Maj. Christopher Wray, *Standing Fast: The Development of German Defensive Doctrine, Prewar to Spring 1943* (Fort Leavenworth: U.S. Army Command and Staff College, 1986).

10. Edgar Röhricht, *Probleme der Kesselschlacht* (Karlsruhe: Kondor, 1958), 30; Franz Halder, *Kriegestagebuch* (Stuttgart: W. Kohlhammer, 1964) 6:181, 209.

11. Jonathan House and David Glantz, *When Titans Clashed: How the Red Army Stopped Hitler* (Lawrence: University of Kansas Press, 1995); David Glantz, *Soviet Defensive Tactics at Kursk, July 1943* (Fort Leavenworth, KS: Combat Studies Institute, U.S. Army Command and General Staff College, 1986); and *Soviet Military Deception in the Second World War* (London: Frank Cass, 1989).

12. Guderian, *Panzer Leader*, 122–4.

13. Macksey, *Panzer General*, 171.

14. On the commissar order in general, see among others, Helmut Krausnick, "Kommissarbefehl und 'Massenexekution' sowjetischer Kriegsgefangener," in *Anatomie des SS-Staates*, ed. Hans Buchelm (Munich: Verlag DVT, 1967), 2:135–232.

15. Christian Streit, "Soviet POWs in the Hands of the Wehrmacht," in *War of Extermination: The German Military in WWII, 1941–1944*, ed. Hannes Heer and Klaus Naumann (New York: Berghahn Books, 2000), 84.

16. Christian Gerlach, "Men of 20 July and the War in the Soviet Union," in Heer and Naumann, *War of Extermination*, 130.

17. Guderian, *Panzer Leader*, 125–26.

18. Bartov, *Hitler's Army*, 86–7.

19. BA-MA RH 22/155, OKH/Gen.Qu., "Regelung des Einsatzes der Sicherheitspolizei und des SD in Verband des Heeres," 28.4.1941 cited in Gerd Überschär and Wolfram Wette, *Der deutsche Überfall auf die Sowjetunion* (Frankfurt: Fischer Taschenbuch 1999), 249ff.

20. Christian Streit, *Keine Kameraden: Die Wehrmacht und die sowjetischen Kriegsgefangenen, 1941–45* (Bonn: Verlag J.H.W. Dietz, 1997), 111.

21. Streit, *Keine Kameraden*, 111.

22. Louis Rotundo, "The Creation of Soviet Reserves and the 1941 Campaign," *Military Affairs*, 50, no. 1 (Jan. 1986), 23ff.

23. Russell Hart, *Clash of Arms: How the Allies Won in Normandy* (Boulder, CO: Lynne Rienner Press, 2000), 204.
24. Macksey, *Panzer General*, 141–2.
25. Koch, review of Macksey's *Guderian: Panzer General*, 4.
26. Ibid.
27. Macksey, *Panzer General*, 143.
28. Ibid., 145.
29. Klaus Gerbet, ed., *Generalfeldmarschall Fedor von Bock: The War Diaries, 1939–1945*, translated by David Johnston (Atglen, PA: Schiffer, 2000), 298, 301, 303–04.
30. Macksey, *Panzer General*, 151–2.
31. Bradley, *Generaloberst Guderian*, 229.
32. Gerbet, *Bock War Diaries*, 338.
33. Ibid., 381.
34. Some three quarters of Guderian's forces were concentrated astride Tula and only four divisions defended his long right flank. David Glantz, *Barbarossa: Hitler's Invasion of Russia, 1941* (Stroud: Tempus, 2001), 199.
35. Earl F. Ziemke and Magna Bauer, *Moscow to Stalingrad: Decision in the East* (Washington, DC: Office of the Chief of Military History, U.S. Army, 1987), 73.
36. Gerbet, *Bock War Diaries*, 382–3.
37. Ibid., 391.
38. Gerbet, *Bock War Diaries*, 393–4, 398.
39. Walter Gorlitz, ed. *The Memoirs of Field Marshal Wilhelm Keitel, Chief of the German High Command, 1938–1945* (New York: Cooper Square Press, 2000), 167.
40. Macksey, *Panzer General*, 160.
41. Wray, *Standing Fast*, chapter 3.
42. Ibid., 69.
43. The number of supply trains reaching their destinations on the Eastern Front declined from 2093 in September 1941 to 1420 in January 1942. Wray, *Standing Fast*, 74.
44. Gerbet, *Bock War Diaries*, 394.
45. Fretter-Pico, *Missbrauchte Infanterie*, 66–7.
46. Ibid.
47. Guderian, *Panzer Leader*, 210.
48. Wray, *Standing Fast*, 73.

Chapter 7
1. On Hitler's bribing of senior officers, see Olaf Groehler, "Die Güter

der Generale: Dotationen im zweiten Weltkrieg," *Zeitschrift für Geschichtswissenschaft (DDR)*, 19, nr. 5 (1971), 655–63; Gerhard Weinberg, *Germany, Hitler, and World War II* (Cambridge: Cambridge University Press, 1995), 308–9; and Norman Goda, "Black Marks: Hitler's Bribery of His Senior Officers," conference presentation, German Studies Association Annual Meeting 1997.

2. Koch, review of Macksey, *Panzer General*, 2.

3. Ibid.

4. For details and documentation regarding Guderian's acquisition of Gut Deipenhof, see National Archives Records Administration microfilm series T-74, roll 7.

5. Goda, "Black Marks," 1 and 6.

6. On German wartime military pay and supplemental payments, see Rudolf Absolon, *Die Wehrmacht im Dritten Reich* (Boppard am Rhein: Boldt, 1969–1995), 5:343–68.

7. Peter Meroth, "Vorschuß auf den Endsieg," *Stern* (1980), 86–92.

8. Goda, "Black Marks," 6.

9. Ibid., 1–2.

10. Ibid., 7–8.

11. Gerhard Weinberg, "Some Thoughts on World War II," in *Germany, Hitler, and World War II*, Gerhard Weinberg, ed., 308–09.

12. I owe this insight to Professor Williamson Murray, visiting professor of Naval Heritage and History, U.S. Naval Academy, Annapolis, MD.

13. Macksey, *Panzer General*, 164.

14. Rudolf Schmundt, *Tätigkeitsbericht des Chefs den Heerespersonalamts, 1 Oktober 1942–29 Oktober 1944* (Osnabrück: Biblio Verlag, 1984), entry for 28 February 1943.

15. For Guderian's opposition, see *Panzer Leader*, 216–22.

16. Fleischer, *Die deutsche Panzerjägertruppe*, 115.

17. On 31 December 1943, 177 StuGs had been allocated to army and SS panzer units in Western Europe. Jentz, *Panzer Truppen*, 2:73.

18. Six panzer and eight panzergrenadier divisions received assault guns during the summer and fall of 1943. Jentz, *Panzer Truppen*, 2:69–70; Fleischer, *Deutschen Sturmgeschützen* (Wölfersheim-Berstadt: Podzun-Pallas, 1996), 97.

19. For improvements in tank inventory record keeping, see NARA T-78, rolls 164–9, OKH, Heereswaffenamt, "Überblick über den Rüstungsstand des Heeres (Waffen und Geräte), 1940–1945."

20. Lochner, *Goebbels Diaries*, 279.

21. Koch, review of Macksey, *Panzer General,* 2.

22. Hartmut Knittel, *Panzerfertigung im Zweiten Weltkrieg. Industrieproduktion für die deutsche Wehrmacht* (Herford: Ernst Mittler und Sohn, 1988), vol. 2, passim.

23. U.S. Dept. of the Army, [Burkhart Müller-Hillebrand], *German Tank Maintenance in World War II* (Washington DC: Center for Military History, 1952), passim.

24. Macksey, *Panzer General,* 176–7.

25. Richard Hallion, *Strike From the Sky: The History of Battlefield Air Attack, 1911–1945* (Washington, DC: Smithsonian Institute Press, 1989), chapter 4; Christopher Calhoun, *German Anti-armor Operations on the Eastern Front: Lessons for Tomorrow's Army* (Carlisle, PA: U.S. Army War College, 1987).

26. Macksey, *Panzer General,* 177.

27. Niklas Zetterling and Anders Frankson, eds., *Kursk, 1943: A Statistical Analysis* (London: Frank Cass, 2000).

28. Hart, *Clash of Arms,* 218.

29. U.S. War Department, *German Military Intelligence* (Frederick, MD: University Publications of America, 1984).

30. For information on Guderian's opposition to self-propelled artillery see his *Panzer Leader,* 216–22.

31. Heinz Guderian, *Die Panzertruppen und ihr Zusammenwirken mit den anderen Waffen* (Berlin: Ernst Mittler und Sohn, 1943), 47.

32. Richard Muller, *The German Air War in Russia* (Baltimore, MD: Nautical and Aviation Publishing Co., 1992), 22.

33. The first Flakpanzer 38t was designed by the 12th SS Panzer Division in the field. Later, improved models of flakpanzers mounted a 37mm medium cannon or, the more deadly, four-barreled 20mm Flakvierling. This proved to be a formidable defensive weapon. Uwe Feist, *Sturmartillerie: Self-Propelled Guns and Flak Tanks* (Fallbrook, CA: Aero Books, 1967), passim.

34. Percy Schramm, ed., *Kriegstagebuch des Oberkommandos der Wehrmacht,* (Frankfurt am Main: Bernard und Graefe, 1909–69) vol. 4; Kurt Mehner, ed., *Die Geheimen Tagesberichte der deutschen Wehrmachtführung im Zweiten Weltkrieg, 1939–1945* (Osnabrück: Biblio, 1984), vols. 11–12; Helmut Heiber and David Glantz, *Hitler's Generals: Military Conferences, 1942–1945* (New York: Enigma Books, 2003).

Chapter 8

1. Fabian von Schlabrendorff, *Offiziere Gegen Hitler* (Europa, 1946), translated by Hilda Simon as *The Secret War Against Hitler* (New York: Pitman, 1965).
2. Guderian, *Panzer Leader*, 1967), 239–41.
3. Macksey, *Panzer General*, 182–4.
4. Ibid., 182.
5. Guderian, *Panzer Leader*, 268–74.
6. Peter Padfield, *Himmler: Reichsführer-SS* (New York: Holt, 1990), 491.
7. Macksey, *Panzer General*, 183.
8. Guderian, *Panzer Leader*, 268–9.
9. Ibid.
10. Macksey, *Panzer General*, 185
11. Geoffrey Megargee, *Inside Hitler's High Command* (Lawrence: University of Kansas Press, 2000), 464.
12. Megargee, *Inside Hitler's High Command*, 464.

Chapter 9

1. Guderian, *Erinnerungen eines Soldaten* (Heidelberg, Kurt Vowinckel, 1951), 307.
2. Walter Warlimont, *Inside Hitler's Headquarters* (Novato, CA: Presidio, 1991), 464–5.
3. Megargee, *Inside Hitler's High Command*, chapter 11.
4. Macksey, *Panzer General*, 192.
5. Warlimont, *Inside Hitler's Headquarters*, 465–6.
6. On Guderian's military role in 1944–45, see Heinrich Schwendemann, "Strategie der Selbstvernichtung: Die Wehrmachtführung im 'Endkampf' um das Dritte Reich," in *Die Wehrmacht: Mythos und Realität* ed. Rolf-Dieter Müller and Hans-Erich Volkmann, (Munich: Oldenbourg, 1999), 224–4.
7. Guderian, *Panzer Leader*, 274–5.
8. Megargee, *Inside Hitler's High Command*, 215.
9. Macksey, *Panzer General*, 189.
10. Ibid.
11. Megargee, *Inside Hitler's High Command*, 214.
12. Ibid., 213.
13. Ibid.
14. Ibid., 216–19.
15. Alfred Mierzejewski, *The Collapse of the German War Economy,*

1944–1945 (Chapel Hill, NC.: University of North Carolina Press, 1988), passim.

16. Megargee, *Inside Hitler's High Command*, 218–19.
17. Schwendemann, "Strategie der Selbstvernichtung," 228.
18. David Yelten. *Hitler's Volkssturm: The Nazi Militia and the Fall of Germany, 1944–1945*, (Lawrence: University of Kansas Press, 2002), 49.
19. Macksey, *Panzer General*, 192.
20. Padfield, *Himmler*, 556.
21. Erich Murawski, *Die Eroberung Pommerns durch die Rote Armee* (Boppard am Rhein: Harald Boldt Verlag, 1969), 158–70.
22. Murawski, *Die Eroberung Pommerns*, 171–277.
23. In one German tank production factory in June 1943 some 47 percent of its workers were foreign slave laborers. Knittel, *Panzerfertigung*, 2:54.
24. Macksey, *Panzer General*, 201.
25. Ibid., 202.
26. Goda, "Black Marks," 9.

Chapter 10
1. Guderian wrote nine separate reports. Headquarters, U.S. Army Europe, Historical Division, *Supplement Guide to Foreign Military Studies, 1945–1954* (Headquarters, U.S. Army Europe, 1959), 244.
2. Transcript of tape-recorded prison conversations between Generals Leeb, von Schweppenburg, and Guderian. Record group 238, roll 31, frames 1157–62, National Archives and Records Administration, Washington, DC. I am grateful to Geoff Megargee for this information.
3. Macksey, *Panzer General*, 207–208.
4. Ibid., 210.
5. Macksey, *Panzer General*, 211; Megargee, *Inside Hitler's High Command*, passim.
6. Macksey, *Panzer General*, 211.
7. The best assessment of Hitler's worldview can be found in Eberhard Jäckel's, *Hitler's Weltanschauung: A Blueprint for Power* (Middletown, CT: Wesleyan University Press, 1972), translated by Herbert Arnold.
8. Macksey, *Panzer General*, 215.

Bibliographic Note

Much has been written about Heinz Guderian, but the number of valuable biographies is actually rather limited. This brief bibliographic note provides a short synopsis of some of the major biographical treatments of Guderian. Space precludes discussion of all of the valuable scholarship cited in the notes. All biographical studies have been heavily influenced by Guderian's own self-serving and distorted memoirs, *Erinnerungen eines Soldaten (Recollections of a Soldier)* (1951), translated into English under the title *Panzer Leader* (1952). Before its publication, Malte Plattenburg had already published an early German language memoir, *Guderian* (1950). Other German-language biographies that have presented sympathetic views of Guderian include Karl Walde's *Guderian* (1976) and Fred Frank's *Heinz Guderian* (1985). Probably the most solid German study is Dermot Bradley's *Generaloberst Heinz Guderian* (1978).

John Keegan provided a commendable biography, *Guderian*, in the famous Ballantine War Leader book series in 1973, but it was a study that rested overwhelmingly on Guderian's own self-image as articulated in *Panzer Leader*. Probably the most popular English-language biography of Guderian is Kenneth Macksey's *Guderian: Creator of the Blitzkrieg* (1975), which he republished in slightly revised form as *Guderian: Panzer General* (1992). While they are both excellent biographies, Macksey, even in his revised biography, presents too flattering a view of Guderian. From the 1980s on, a slew of new German and English-language studies of the Second World War have increasingly illuminated the exaggeration and distortion that mar *Panzer Leader*. Valuable studies that shed new light on Guderian's more limited role in creating Germany's armored force in the 1930s include Robert Citino's *The Path to Blitzkrieg* (1987) and James Corum's *The Road to Blitzkrieg* (1992). Hubertus Senff's article "Entwicklung der Panzerwaffe" (1969) also demonstrates the simplistic view Guderian portrayed of the institutional "turf wars" of that period. Excellent studies by Gerhard Weinberg (1995) and Norman Goda (1997), among others, have proven that Guderian took massive bribes from Hitler that he "forgot" to mention in his autobiography.

Other operational studies have placed Guderian's actual combat successes in more accurate relief. Among these are Lassner's (2000) article on the catastrophe that befell Guderian's 2d Panzer Division in its unopposed occupation of Austria in 1938. Florian Rothbrust's excellent analysis, *Guderian's XIX Corps and the Battle for France* (1990) reveals the careful planning and intense training that contributed to the successful penetration of the Ardennes. On Guderian's tenure as Acting Chief of the General Staff during 1944–45, important insight is provided by Geoffrey Megargee's *Inside Hitler's High Command* (2000). Both it and Heinrich Schwendemann's article "Strategie der Selbstvernichtung" (1999) reveal Guderian to be as myopic, fanatical, and indifferent to human death and misery as his beloved Führer.

Index

About the Author

Russell A. Hart is Associate Professor of History at Hawai'i Pacific University on Oahu in Hawai'i. He is a specialist in the history of the Second World War in the European theater. He received his B.A. (Hons) from the University of Durham, England, and his MA and PhD from the Ohio State University. He is author of *Clash of Arms: How the Allies Won in Normandy*, as well as five coauthored books: *German Tanks of WWII* (1998); *Equipment and Fighting Tactics of the Waffen-SS* (1999); *Panzer: The Illustrated History of Germany's Armored Forces in World War II* (1999); *The German Soldier in World War II* (2000); and *The Second World War, Part Six: Northwest Europe, 1944–1945* (2002). He lives in Kailua, Hawai'i.